Used with kind permission of WaltonCreative.com

Carolyn Forster is a best-selling quilting author, with over 175,000 books sold worldwide. She started making quilts when she was a teenager, and her passion for patchwork and quilting led her to study Textiles at Bath Spa University, UK. Since then, she has taught patchwork and quilting both in the UK and the USA and has had her quilts featured in a number of books and magazines, including Today's Quilter and French magazine Magic Patch. Carolyn lives in Tunbridge Wells, UK.

www.carolynforster.co.uk | @quiltingonthego

The original best-selling Twenty to Make *series has sold over 2 million copies worldwide! In a handy hardback pocket-size format that makes them perfect little gifts, each title in the* All-New Twenty to Make *series contains 20 brand-new projects.*

Like this book? Here are some more in this series:

9781800922587

9781800922518

9781800920989

9781800921467

9781800920873

9781800921399

9781800921009

9781800921603

ALL-NEW 20 TO MAKE

To discover more in the *All-New 20 to Make* series, scan the QR code, right.

ALL-NEW

20 TO MAKE

CHICKEN SCRATCH EMBROIDERY

Carolyn Forster

SEARCH PRESS

First published in 2026

Search Press Limited
Wellwood, North Farm Road,
Tunbridge Wells, Kent TN2 3DR

1 2 3 4 5 6 7 8 9 10

Photographs by Stacy Grant
Illustrations and diagrams by Bess Harding

ISBN: 978-1-80092-355-3
ebook ISBN: 978-1-80093-338-5

Bookmarked Hub
For further ideas and inspiration, and to join our free online community, visit www.bookmarkedhub.com

Publishers' notes
Imperial measurements are used in this book; the metric conversions are rounded to the nearest 0.25cm. Always use either metric or imperial measurements, not a combination of both.

The Publishers and author can accept no responsibility for any consequences arising from the information, advice or instructions given in this publication.

GPSR information can be found at www.searchpress.com

Printed in China, AP102025

FSC www.fsc.org
MIX
Paper | Supporting responsible forestry
FSC® C136333

CONTENTS

INTRODUCTION

Over the last 100 or so years, embroidery on gingham – often known as chicken scratch embroidery, broderie suisse, snowflake embroidery, Amish lace, Depression lace and Hoover lace – has captured the imagination of stitchers all over the world. There's something about the simple stitches and their lace-like effects that allows the fresh, bright colours of gingham to shine through. It's this effect that – despite the different names this embroidery goes by, and its roller-coaster journey through stitching trends over the years – has kept this classic form of stitchery around for so long.

Gingham embroidery is an easy way to decorate and personalize your home textiles, as well as clothing. All that's required are a few simple stitches, your chosen thread and a checked fabric to stitch on. Besides being accessible, gingham embroidery is also portable and extremely meditative: you can store the embroidery in a small bag while travelling and stitch on the go, and the easy, almost repetitive stitching means you can sit and let your thoughts wander, but keep your hands busy and have a charming product at the end.

We will first look at some of the basic stitches you'll need, plus the variations you can create with them by adding techniques like weaving. Then, there are 20 designs to embroider. Throughout the embroideries section, you'll see the kinds of items you can embroider with chicken scratch; however, don't be afraid to use the design on a different accessory, garment or homeware. And as you stitch one design, you may wonder what it would look like in different colours, on different checks – or perhaps on a completely different fabric!

It's very easy to dive into a rabbit hole of creativity with gingham embroidery, and it's this adaptability that ensures it will continue to be a popular technique for many more years to come.

Carolyn

For more about Carolyn and her work, visit:

- her website: www.carolynforster.co.uk
- her Instagram page: @quiltingonthego

MATERIALS AND TOOLS

GINGHAM

There's a tendency to focus on the stitches in chicken scratch embroidery, but of course the technique wouldn't exist without gingham – a medium-weight even-weave fabric usually made from cotton or cotton blends.

BACKGROUND

But why is gingham used?

Gingham was introduced to Europe in the 17th century via Malaysia, and its name can be traced back to the Malay word 'genggang', meaning separate or striped. Originally a striped fabric, the way gingham was produced in factories around the mid-18th century led to it changing to the now recognizable three-tone, checked design. After the Victorian era, gingham was always checked. The fabric was popular in France too, and there it was renamed 'Vichy' after the town that produced it – and is still known by this in many countries today. Vichy fabric is mostly woven in blue and white.

Gingham was a cheap fabric to produce, so it experienced a resurgence in popularity during the 1930s and 1940s, when many countries were struggling economically before and after the Second World War. This 'make do and mend' era meant techniques like chicken scratch embroidery were used to add interest and enhance cheaper fabrics – for example, in the USA during the 1930s, the fashion-conscious used embroidery to embellish basic fabric for garments. Hence why chicken scratch is sometimes known as 'Depression lace'.

The checked appearance of gingham also makes it easy to count stitches and so, in a sense, chicken scratch embroidery could be considered a distant cousin to other counted embroidery techniques like cross stitch.

A NOTE ON CORDED GINGHAM

Most gingham is woven with the same number of threads in each direction but you can get corded gingham, which has a slight ridge (of denser threads) either side of the checks (**A**). This shouldn't pose a problem when sewing, but is worth noting in case you wonder why it seems slightly different.

SQUARE SIZES

The squares in gingham can range in size, from ⅛in (approx. 2mm) up to 1in (2.5cm) square (**B**). I tend use ¼in (5mm) gingham squares (or close to that size), as it's not only what's been used traditionally but I also prefer its appearance.

However, the nature of gingham embroidery makes it easy to scale the stitching up or down, so you can have fun making the designs in this book on smaller or larger gingham squares, if that's your preference. Note that if your gingham squares are smaller or larger than the ones I've used in the book, the look of your finished embroidery will be different to mine.

If you decide to use a gingham fabric with larger squares, you may need to use thicker threads. I'd recommend experimenting with thread sizes on a scrap of your chosen gingham, to test whether the thread suits it. For example, on a 1in (2.5cm) square gingham, I will use all six strands of stranded floss, while on ¼in (5mm) gingham I use three strands.

Important note: Before buying or stitching it, it's worth looking closely at your chosen gingham to check the shapes of its squares, as sometimes they're not as square as you might assume. If this is the case, just make sure you have a constant for the top and bottom of the work if you are using panels together in a project.

USING ALTERNATIVE FABRICS

Despite the name, you don't actually need a gingham background for your gingham embroidery! Applying your designs to other fabrics opens up lots of possibilities with your stitching, giving the design a whole new look compared to the pieces we see from the 1930s.

Printed checks (C) are one option, and they can be a fun alternative if words are printed on the fabric, too, since they can be incorporated into the design. Note printed checks don't always follow the straight grain of the fabric and some have a more painterly effect too. However, if the squares are slightly wonky, just run with it for a fun effect!

Smocking transfer dots (D): You can buy sheets of dots, available in various sizes, to iron onto fabric. Intended for smocking stitches, smocking dots act like the squares of gingham fabric, so it's easy to translate a gingham-embroidery design to a grid made from smocking dots. The dots will disappear when the fabric is soaked (although it's worth checking that the dots wash out of a sample piece of your fabric before stitching). Usually I cut the paper to the shape of my stitched design, so there are fewer dots and less wastage.

Waste canvas (E): This is a starched mesh grid that can be pinned or basted / tacked to the right side of any fabric, and then stitched over. Once the embroidery is complete, the mesh is soaked with a damp cloth to dissolve the starch; the threads can then be pulled away easily. The grid comes in a selection of sizes, which means you can choose the size of your 'squares', just like you would if using actual gingham fabric. Since the canvas is stiff, I don't like to use a hoop when stitching with it initially: I stitch all the main chicken scratch stitches and any lines where I need the grid of the canvas to aid me; if there are any weaving stitches, it's then that I remove the canvas to complete these. At this point, I'll also put the work in a hoop to keep it flat.

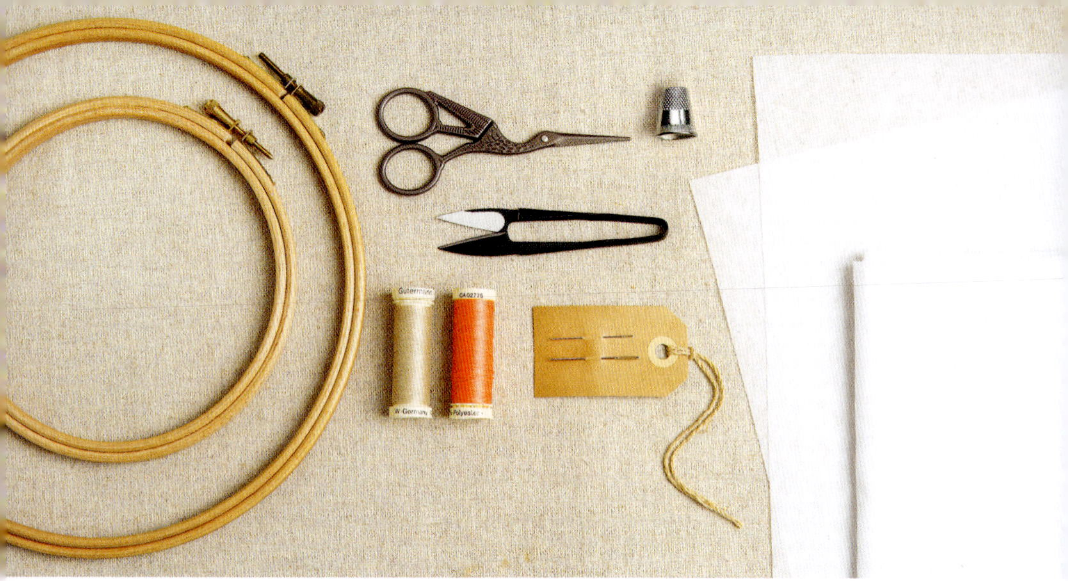

INTERFACINGS AND STABILIZERS

Some fabrics that you stitch on will feel sturdy enough to handle and for the project you wish to make; others may seem a little flimsy and need a bit of backing to support them.

For fabrics that I think would benefit from some extra structure, I use an iron-on interfacing. My favourite is Vlieseline G710, which is a lightweight woven interfacing that comes in black or white. Once adhered to the wrong side of your fabric, it keeps the fabric firm but does not affect how it's handled or stitched.

If you just want to stabilize a small area, rather than the whole piece of fabric, look at using a tear-away stabilizer. I like to use Vlieseline's Stitch-n-Tear. Like a regular stabilizer, this is attached to the wrong side of the work – just pin then baste / tack it in place behind the area you wish to stitch. When I use tear-away stabilizer, often I leave it in the work, perhaps just trimming it down to a smaller area after I've finished embroidering.

SCISSORS AND SNIPS

Thread snips or small scissors are best for cutting the threads as they are easy to handle and sharp.

NEEDLES

I use size 6 embroidery needles for stitching. When weaving your stitches, it is best to use the eye of the needle and push from the pointed end; this prevents you from unwittingly snagging your stitches. I recommend using your thimble for this! If pushing from the pointed end makes you nervous, use a tapestry needle size 22 instead, so that you are pushing a blunted needle tip rather than a sharp one.

EMBROIDERY HOOPS

Holding your work in a frame while you embroider stops you pulling the stitches too tight, giving you a nice flat result. Since I like to keep my work flat when I stitch it, I tend to use 6in (15cm) and 8in (20cm) diameter hoops most frequently. If you look at the examples on page 44, you can see the little hoops I worked them in became the final frames for those stitcheries too.

BASTING / TACKING THREAD

For stitching the central marking lines on the gingham to help place the design (see page 20).

EMBROIDERY THREADS

According to different pattern sources from the 1960s, cotton perle was a popular recommendation for gingham embroidery, as was stranded floss. Often the user was told to use the full six strands; however, typically these patterns featured a single cross stitch, so it makes sense a thicker thread was suggested, to give the best impact for the stitch and design.

Traditionally, the thread colour used was the same as either the light or dark squares of the gingham, accentuating the lacy effect of the stitches on the fabric. For example, broderie suisse work typically uses red and white fabric, so red and white threads are used for its stitching to match. However, and as you'll see in some of the examples in this book, you can add many more shades and even select colours that are not in the gingham. A favourite gingham I work on is quite neutral, so makes the ideal blank canvas on which to add colour. These colours are sometimes drawn from other printed fabrics in the item it's stitched on. Or, sometimes it's just what feels right – if you look at the pincushion on page 46, I selected a bright thread that contrasted wonderfully with the teal gingham.

STRANDED COTTON FLOSS

Stranded floss (**A**) is what was used traditionally for gingham embroidery as it was readily available and economical as well. You can sew with all six strands, but I like to split it into two sets of three strands. Have a practice to see which effect you like to work with. Stranded floss comes in so many colours that there will be something to suit all palettes; there are also variegated types too, so you can have a blend of colours or shades all within one thread.

ALTERNATIVES

Sometimes it is nice to try something new, and see how different threads will look on the work. Really there are no rules, and if you like working with a particular thread and the results it gives, then go right ahead.

Some threads you could use are:

- solid sashiko thread (**B**)
- variegated sashiko thread (**C**)
- cotton perle no. 12 (**D**)
- cotton perle no. 5 (**E**)
- coton à broder no. 16 (**F**)
- Aurifil no. 12 (**G**)
- vintage linen thread (**H**).

STITCH LIBRARY

Part of the appeal of gingham embroidery is the ability to build an increasingly complex design with just a few basic stitches. If you look at stitches used on projects advertised in pamphlets in the 1960s and before, many just used a single cross stitch to create the designs. However, many designs today use a double cross stitch (or Smyrna Stitch) or a quintuple stitch, since they offer a denser stitch, creating more visual impact. For a lace-like effect, you can weave around these basic foundation stitches too.

Important note: generally, the stitches are sewn on either the lightest or darkest squares of the gingham, depending on your design, in order to highlight the pale or dark squares.

MARKING THE FABRIC

Marking the centre of the embroidery on the fabric will help you position the the design on your item successfully, as many of the stitches are influenced by the colours of the squares they're placed in. To mark the fabric, I hand- or machine-sew two lines of large running stitches in both directions – top to bottom and left to right – across the full area of the embroidery with basting / tacking thread. These running stitches are removed once the embroidery is complete.

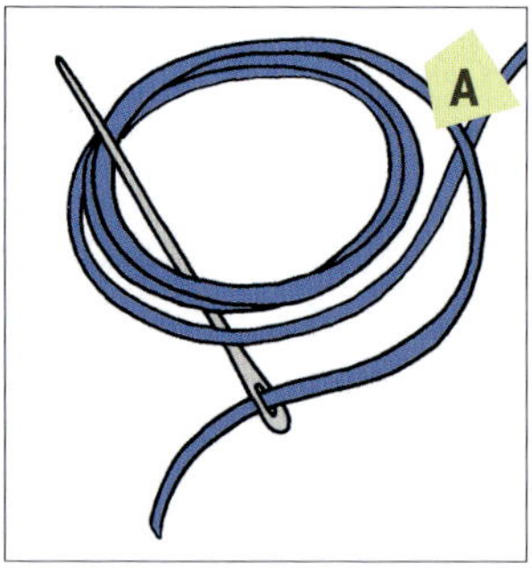

TO START A STITCH

1 Cut a thread as long as your arm – thread that is too long will twist and knot as you work. I like to split stranded floss into two sets of three threads, and work with three strands at a time.

2 Thread the needle and tie a knot in the end. I tie a knot by wrapping the end of the thread around my middle finger three times, then poking the end through this circle (**A**) and pulling the knot tight.

3 Bring the needle up through the fabric from the wrong side to the right side, at the point where you wish to start your stitching.

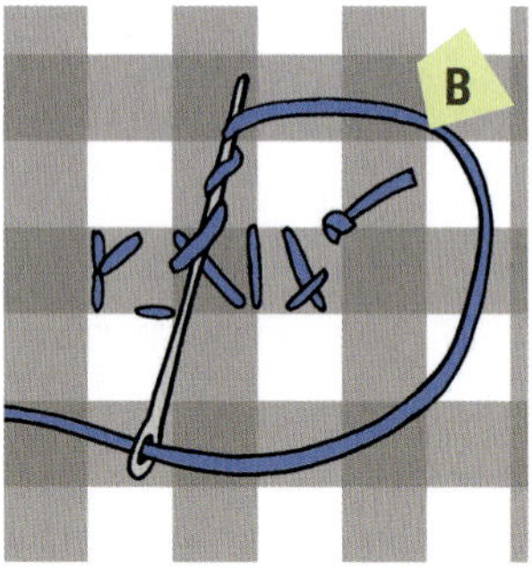

TO FINISH A STITCH

When you are nearing the end of the thread, take the needle through to the back of the work and knot it close to the gingham (**B**). Snip the thread, leaving a ½in (approx. 1cm) tail.

Alternatively, you can fasten off by working two or three buttonhole stitches over some of the threads on the back of the work. Again, I snip the thread, leaving a ½in (approx. 1cm) tail.

⁄ HALF CROSS STITCH (HCS)

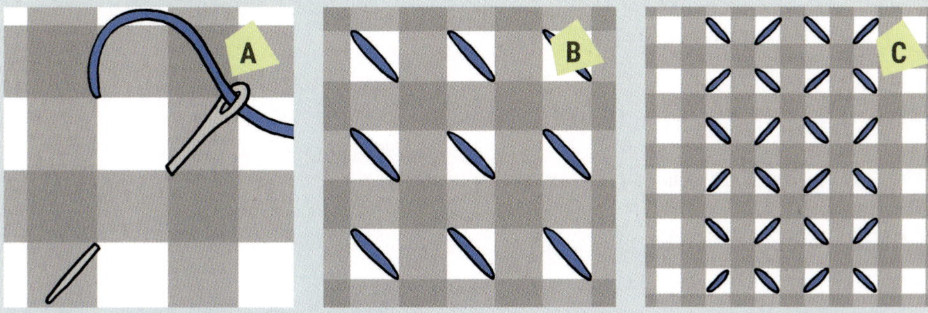

You can work one stitch at a time or work a grid as we have here. It will depend on your project so don't worry about changing your approach. If you are working on something like a heart shape, then this might be sewn as an outline first and then filled in.

Bring the needle up in a top corner of a square, and down diagonally in the opposite bottom corner. One half cross stitch (HCS) made.

If you are working more than one HCS at a time, at the same time as you take the needle down bring it out at the top of the next square (**A**), then repeat as required (**B**). Depending on the design, note that you don't aways have to start in the same top corner (**C**).

× SINGLE CROSS STITCH (SCS)

Make one HCS. Then, bring the needle up at one bottom corner and down at the opposite top corner to complete the single cross stitch (SCS). Note all the second layer of stitches should be worked in the same direction for a consistent look.

To embroider a group of SCS, stitch multiple HCSs as described above first; then, bring the needle out in one free corner of a square containing a HCS, take it down in the remaining free corner of the same square then bring it out in the next free corner of another square, ready to complete the next SCS (**A**). Continue in this way to create a group of SCs quickly (**B**).

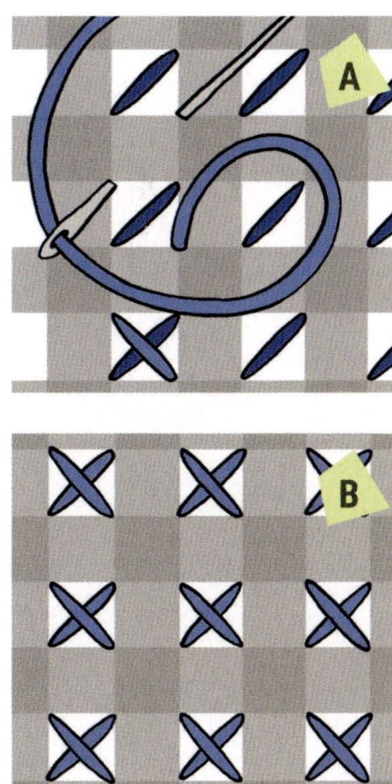

✳ DOUBLE CROSS STITCH (DCS) / SMYRNA STITCH

Repeat the steps for making a SCS as detailed on page 11. Then, you need to work vertical and horizontal stitches over the centre / intersection of the cross stitch (like a mini plus symbol).

As before, the speediest way to stitch is to embroider all in one direction first, then finish with the other direction. It doesn't matter which direction you choose to start with, but it's important you do the same for all the stitches in the design so they look identical to one another, and create a neater finish. For example, once the main cross-stitch shape is established, you could work all the horizontal stitches first (**A**) then end with the vertical stitches (**B**), or vice versa.

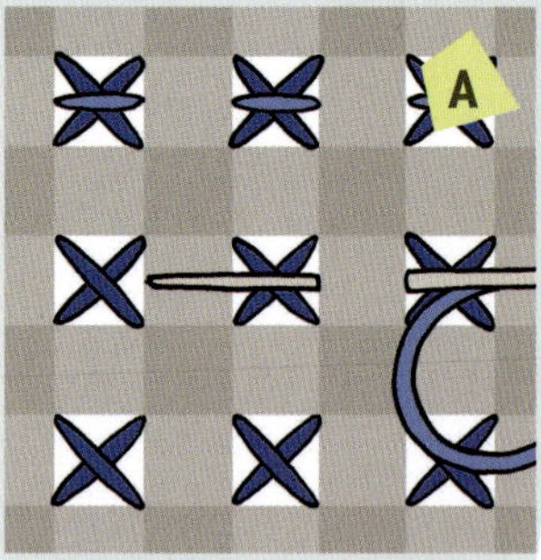

⨳ QUINTUPLE STITCH (QS)

This stitch is one of several variations in the cross-stitch family that is called rice stitch. Since there is also another stitch called rice stitch that is completely different, to avoid confusion I am calling this version 'quintuple stitch' because it forms five crosses. This stitch can often replace the DCS in some designs. It has a denser appearance and adds some nice extra texture too.

Work multiple SCS as detailed on page 11, ensuring the stitches are worked in the same direction.

Now you'll work one stitch at time. First, embroider tiny diagonal stitches over the ends of one half of the cross stitch (**A**). Again, ensure the direction is consistent – bring the needle up from the same top corner and the same opposite bottom corner. Then, fill in the remaining corners, working in a consistent direction as before (**B** and **C**). Repeat as necessary for the rest of the stitches.

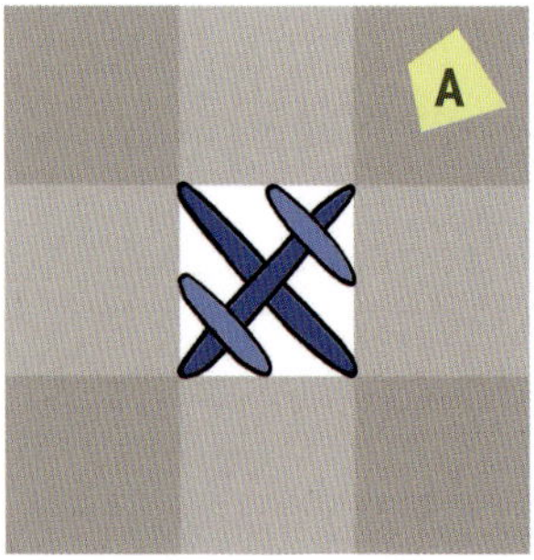

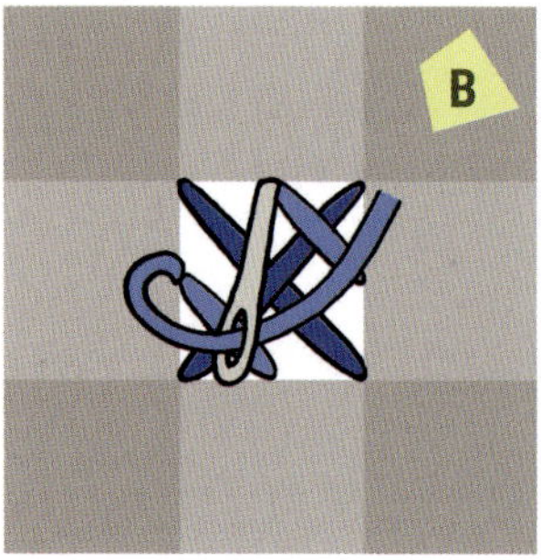

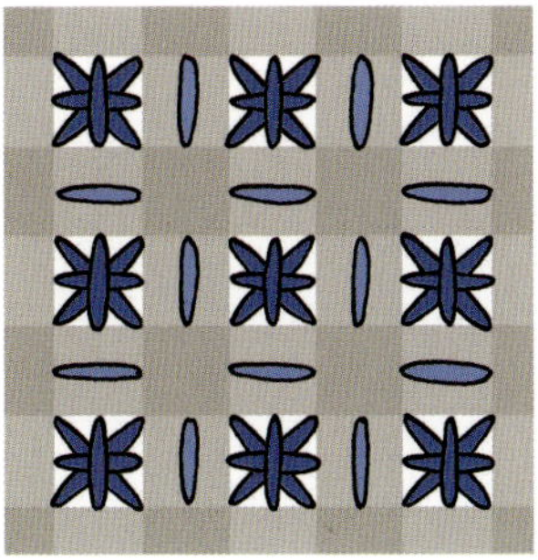

| STRAIGHT STITCH (SS)

Typically, this is worked between DCSs and QSs to create a foundation for woven designs. However, they can be left as is or used in conjunction with French knots (as in the design on page 34). To work a straight stitch (SS), simply bring the needle up from one side of a square, halfway along the edge, then down at the opposite side, again halfway along. To repeat, work all the straight stitches in one direction (e.g. all horizontal stitches first), then embroider all the stitches in the other direction (e.g. all vertical stitches). This means you can embroider them like running stitches, making the process quick and easy.

• FRENCH KNOT (FK)

Bring the needle up at the desired point (usually the centre of the square). Keeping the tension on the thread, wrap the thread around the needle – close to the tip – two to three times (**A**). Maintaining tension, insert the needle into the fabric close to where you started (**B**).

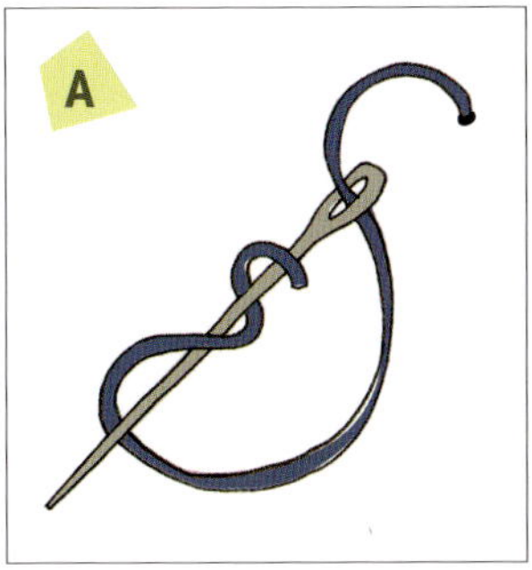

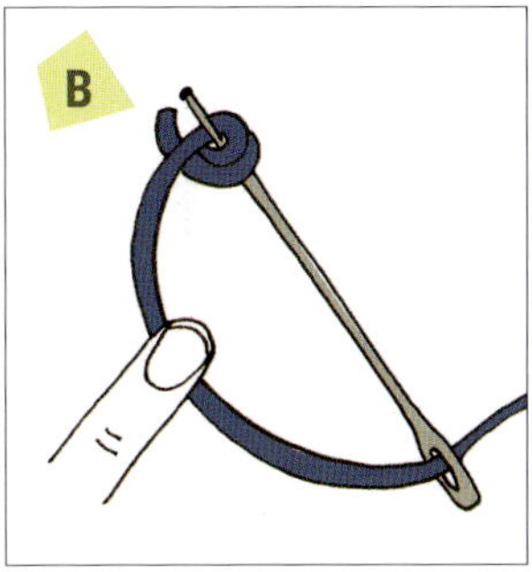

WEAVING

Once foundation stitches are in place (SCSs, DCSs, QSs or SSs), lacy designs can be created by weaving in and out of the stitches with a needle and thread.

I do all my weaving with the eye of the needle, so I am pushing from the pointed end; this is because the blunt end of the needle is less likely to pierce the already stitched threads. I highly recommend wearing a thimble for this! Alternatively, you could use a tapestry needle instead: because it has a blunt point, you can push from the eyelet end of the needle as before but won't have a pointed end that may pierce the threads – or your fingers!

Depending on the design, you can weave one or two 'circuits' for your woven stitches – i.e. you can weave the design either once or twice around the same area. With woven crosses being the exception (as you'll always weave two circuits for each oval in a woven cross), how many circuits you work is entirely up to you and how well it works for the embroidery motif you're stitching. I've suggested the number of circuits in the relevant designs in this book.

The weaving thread can be the same colour as the foundation stitches or in a different shade – it is up to you, and what works with your gingham, other fabrics and the overall design.

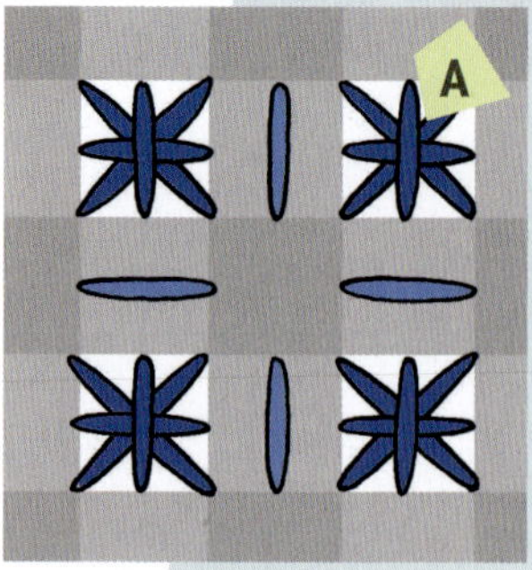

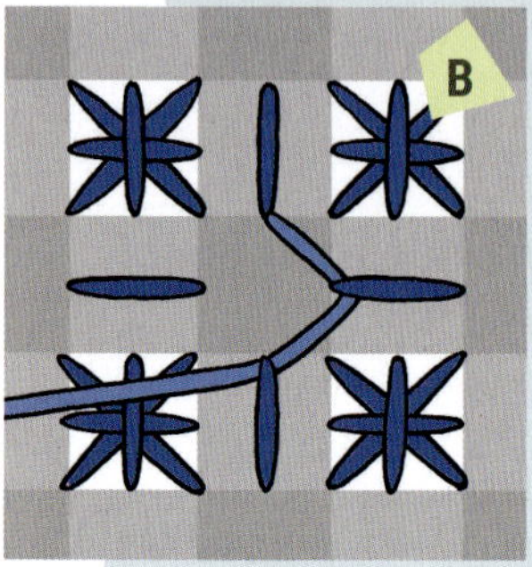

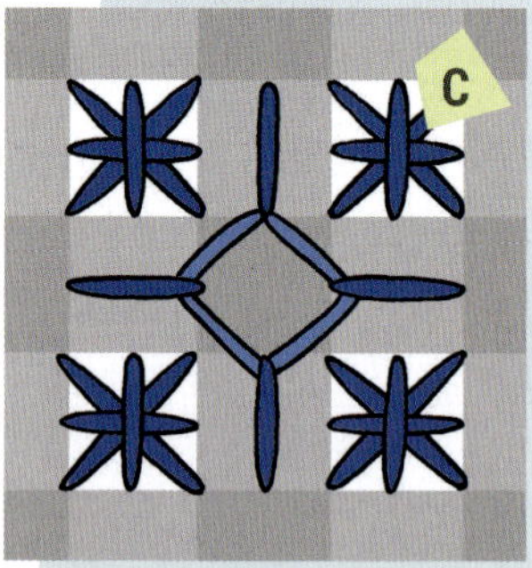

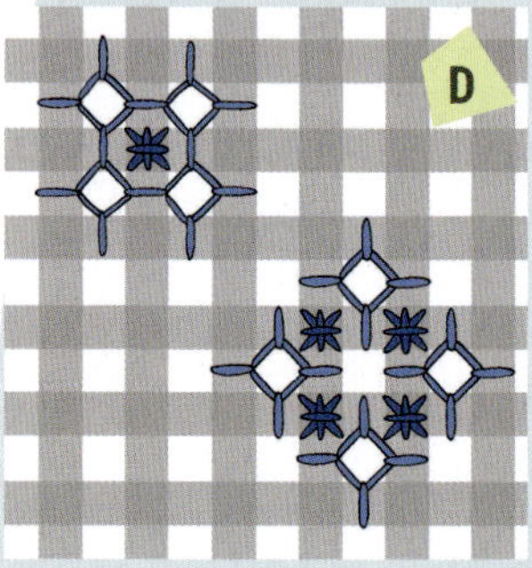

◇ DIAMONDS

1 First, create your base. Over a 3x3 'grid' of gingham squares, stitch two vertical and two horizontal SSs as shown (**A**).

2 Bring the needle up from the wrong side, underneath and at the base of the top vertical SS. Then, use the blunt end of the needle to weave the thread under the left end of the right-hand horizontal stitch, the top end of the bottom vertical stitch (**B**), and then the right end of the left-hand horizontal stitch, creating a diamond. You could repeat the circuit for a stronger effect, but I tend to keep mine to a single weave.

3 To finish, take the needle down at the point where you first came up, at the base of the first stitch (**C**).

4 To add more diamonds, pass the needle along the back of the work and up at your next desired starting point.

5 You can make some very intricate-looking patterns with woven diamonds (**D**). Note the DCSs in these examples are stitched onto the darker squares, so the woven stitches frame the palest squares.

☐ SQUARES

This woven pattern is similar in appearance to the woven diamond opposite, but is woven around the corners of cross stitches or QSs, rather than straight stitches. It's great for outlining and highlighting empty squares in between those with stitches.

1 First, create your base. Over a 3x3 'grid' of gingham squares, stitch a DCS in each corner, leaving the squares in between and the central square empty.

2 For the woven square, bring the needle up underneath and at the end of the bottom-right leg of the top-left DCS. Then weave it under the following: end of the bottom-left leg of the top-right DCS, the end of the top-left leg of the bottom-right DCS, and the end of the top-right leg of the bottom-left DCS. One circuit complete.

3 Make another circuit if desired by taking the needle under the end of the bottom-right leg of the top-left DCS (**A**), follow the path of your first line of weaving all the way around the central square (**B**). Whether you work one round of weaving or two, take the needle down at the starting point.

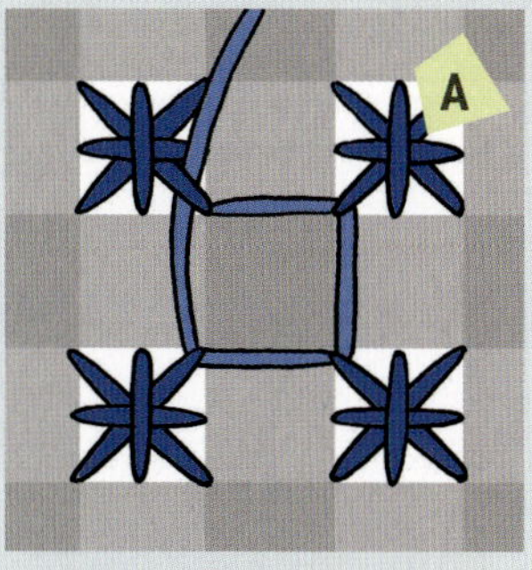

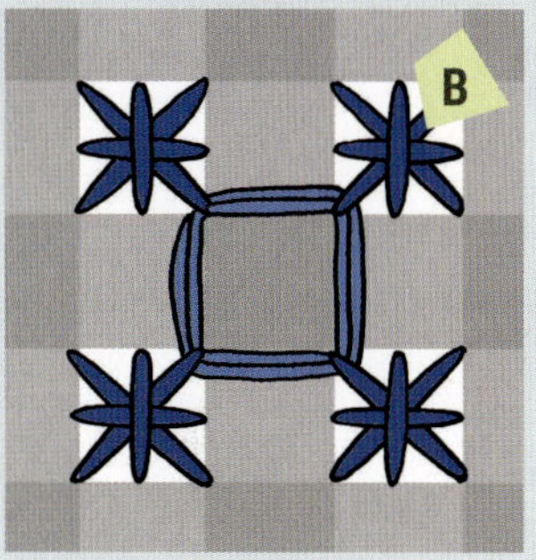

△ TRIANGLES

Triangles are woven almost exactly the same way as woven squares; you leave out one of the four corners of the square, and just weave under three stitches.

OVALS

This weaving pattern creates a strong 'line' in chicken scratch embroidery, neatly linking DCSs. It can be worked individually, and in different directions, but also works well as a border. Weave two circuits for more definition, or just the one circuit for a lighter look.

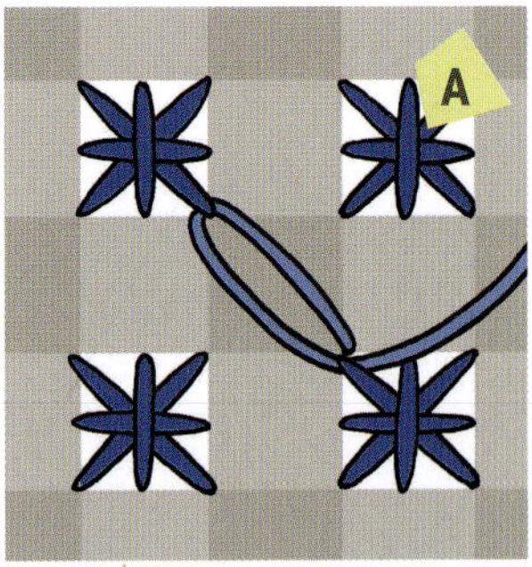

INDIVIDUAL DIAGONAL OVAL STITCHES:

1 You'll need four DCS foundation stitches in a 3x3 'grid' of squares, with a blank square in between each and in the centre.

2 Bring the needle up under and at the end of the top-left leg of the bottom-right DCS. Weave the needle under the end of the bottom-right leg of the top-left DCS then back to your starting point. One oval circuit made.

3 To make a second circuit, weave the needle under the top-left leg of the bottom-right DCS (**A**) and then under the of the bottom-right leg of the top-left DCS once more. To finish, take the needle down at your starting point (**B**).

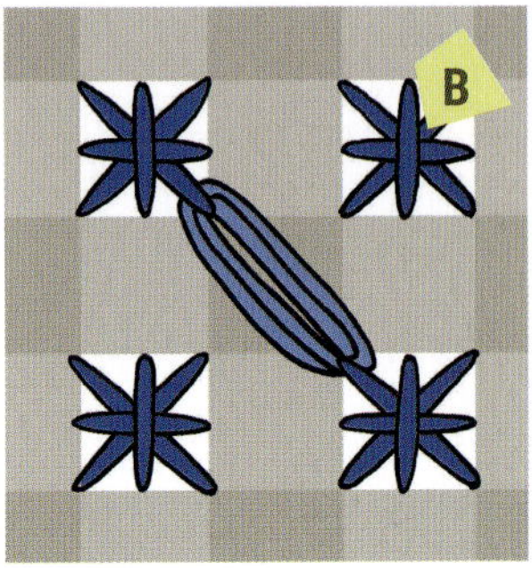

INDIVIDUAL STRAIGHT OVAL STITCHES:

For straight oval stitches, follow a similar process to steps 2 and 3 above, this time bringing the needle up and under the end of a horizontal side leg of a DCS (see right of **C**) or a vertical bottom or top leg of a DCS (see left of **C**) then weave the needle around the central stitch of the opposite DCS. Make a second round of weaving, if desired. Finish in the same way – take the needle down at the starting point.

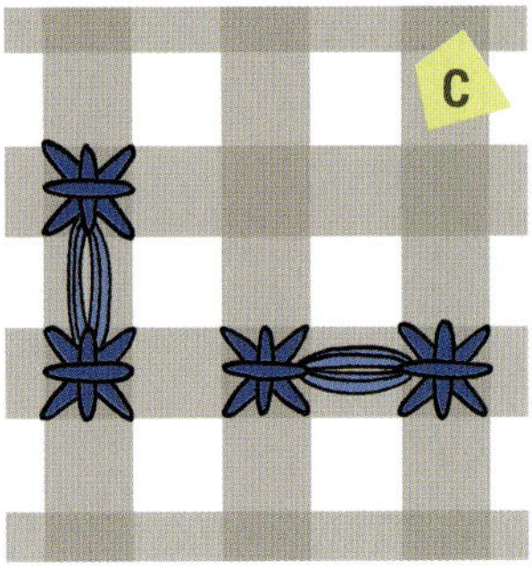

ROW OF STRAIGHT OVAL STITCHES:

1 You'll need a row DCS foundation stitches first, with an empty square in between in each stitch.

2 Bring the needle up under the right-hand end of the horizontal leg of the first DCS. Then, take the needle under the left-hand end of the horizontal leg of the next DCS. Either work another circuit in the same way, or take the needle down at the starting point.

3 Repeat step 2 across the row (**D**).

WOVEN CROSS

This is based on the diagonal oval stitch opposite, but there is a second diagonal woven through the first diagonal oval, creating a cross-like design. Don't be put off, as it's simpler than it looks.

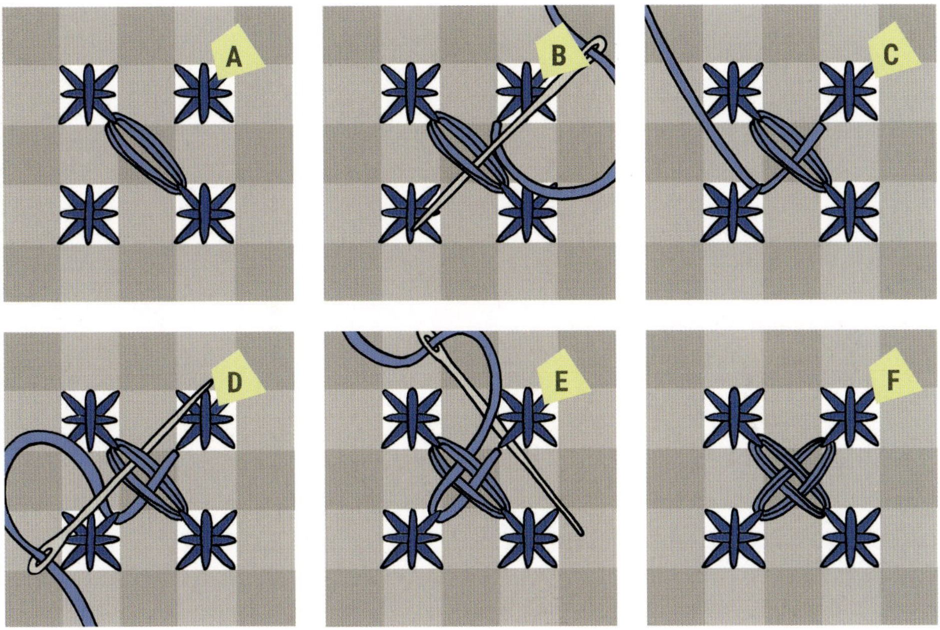

1 You'll need four DCS foundation stitches in a 3x3 'grid' of squares, with a blank square in between each and in the centre.

2 Weave a diagonal oval stitch between the top-left and bottom-right DCSs as described opposite, taking the needle down at the starting point after weaving two circuits (**A**).

3 Start the second diagonal oval stitch by bringing the needle up at the end of the bottom-left leg of the top-right DCS (see **B**).

4 Weave the needle over the right-hand strands of the first diagonal oval stitch, then under the left-hand strands (**B**).

5 Weave the needle under and around the end of the top-right leg of the bottom-left DCS (**C**). Next, take it over the left-hand strands of the first diagonal oval stitch, then under the right-hand strands to bring it back to the starting point (**D**).

6 Weave the needle under and around the end of the bottom-left leg of the top-right DCS to complete the first circuit (**E**).

7 Repeat steps 4 and 5 once more to complete a second circuit. Finish by taking the needle down at the starting point then fastening off on the back. One woven cross made (**F**).

CONTINUOUS LINE

This weaving can be used on any size grid of DCS to create neat straight lines within motifs or for borders. It's made in two stages, whether you use it as a straight line or for a border. I like to use three strands of stranded cotton floss.

INTERTWINED:

Note: If you look closely at the finished design, the cross-over in the weaving is always between the top and bottom DCSs. Keep this in mind when working to keep you on track.

1 Bring the needle up at the corner of a DCS (**A**) and weave through the corner of the opposite DCS (**B**), then along to and around the corner of the next DCS (**C**), up diagonally and around the opposite corner (**D**), and then along to and around the next DCS (**E**); repeat all the way to the end (**J**). First half of the design complete.

2 Take the needle down into the fabric then up at the corner of the opposite DCS (**K**). Repeat the process in step 1, albeit in the opposite direction, overlapping the previous stitching. Take the needle down at the end (**T**) to finish the second side.

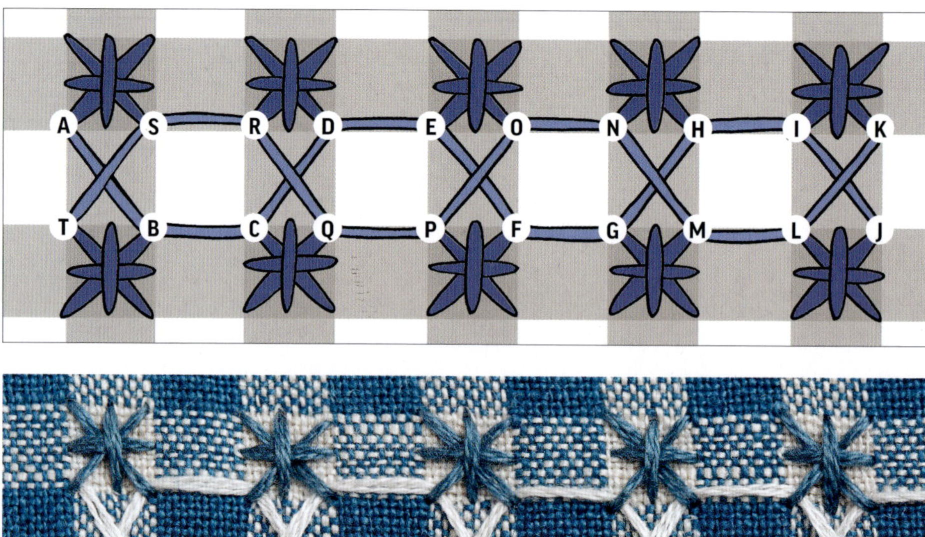

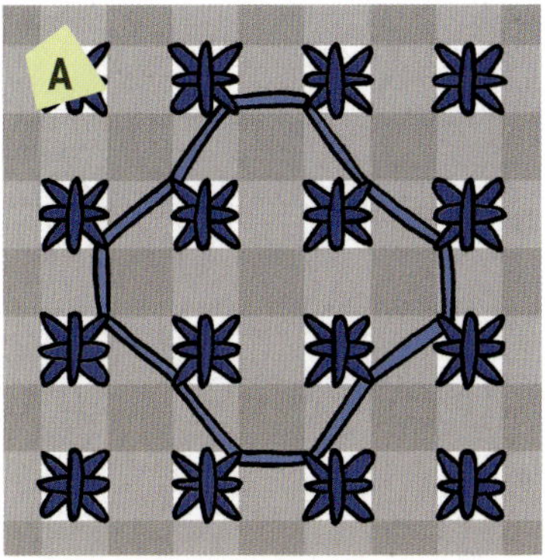

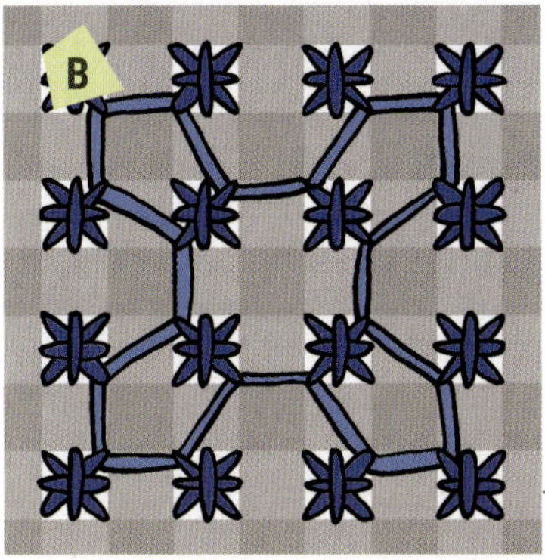

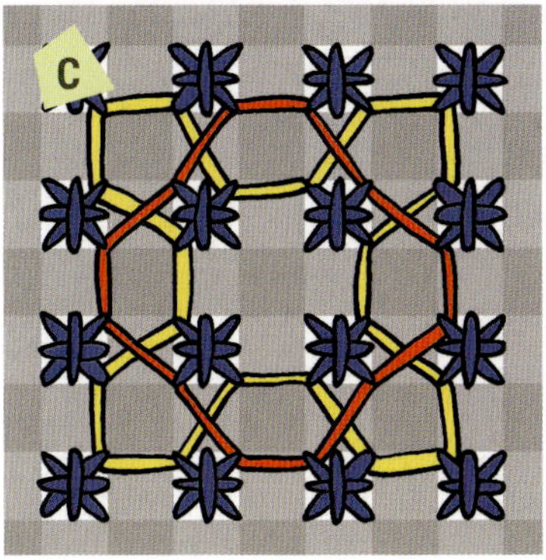

BORDERS:

For a single continuous outline (as in **A** and **B**), simply weave around the appropriate legs of the required DCSs to create your outline. You can complete one or two circuits, depending on the desired effect.

For an intertwined border, as in **C**, work your first outline or circuit (see the yellow outline in **C**), taking the needle down at the end; then, bring the needle up at the beginning of your second circuit and weave your design over the top of your first-circuit stitches (see the red outline in **C**).

EMBROIDERY DESIGNS

BEFORE YOU BEGIN

- 'RS' means 'right side' (i.e. front of the embroidery) and 'WS' means 'wrong side' (i.e. back of the embroidery).
- Always **mark the centre of the embroidery with two lines of running stitches using basting / tacking thread** – top to bottom and left to right – on the RS of the fabric, especially if the project is large. You can do this by hand with a simple running stitch or for speed on the sewing machine. This is an important first step, as these centre lines will help you position the embroidery on your item. These running stitches are removed once the embroidery is complete.
- When the embroidery is finished, cover it with a cloth and **press the embroidery from the WS**; this helps to settle the stitches.
- Throughout this book I've stitched my designs onto items I've made from gingham fabric, but the embroidery can be applied to any item you like! If your item is made from a different kind of checked fabric, this can give your design a more organic appearance. If your base isn't made from any kind of checked fabric, you create your own grid with the help of smocking dots or waste canvas; these can then be soaked away afterwards. See page 7 for more information on these products.
- Each embroidery design includes the following: a diagram of the whole design, a section of it or its repeat; a symbol key that lists the stitches used in the embroidery (see the full list, right); the finished size of the embroidery; requirements for stitching the embroidery; and working instructions. There is also some information about the item the embroidery design was worked on too, for inspiration.
- Unless stated otherwise, **I've used three strands of stranded cotton floss for all the patterns**. The amount of thread is not given, just the colour used. For smaller patterns, you will need only one skein; for larger patterns, you may need two skeins in each colour.
- For **woven stitches**, unless stated otherwise **assume two circuits have been worked**.

SYMBOL KEY

/	HCS (page 11)
×	SCS (page 11)
✳	DCS (page 12)
⋇	QS (page 12)
|	SS (page 13)
●	FK (page 13)
◇	Woven diamonds (page 14)
□	Woven squares (page 15)
△	Woven triangles (page 15)
⬭	Woven ovals (page 16)
⊠	Woven cross (page 17)
⌐	Continuous line (pages 18–19)

KNOT GARDENS

Inspirational makes:
These tiny motifs are perfect on mini items like buttons, rings, coin purses, charms, and – when worked in an alternating, repeating row together – even the neckline around a top.

PATTERN NOTES

The diagrams below show the two Knot Garden motifs – the smaller design features a woven square, and the larger motif features woven triangles.

The small woven square motif is worked over a 3x3 grid of squares, and the larger woven triangles motif is worked over a 5x5 grid of squares.

As these designs are so tiny, you shouldn't need to add running stitch guide lines, and can work by eye.

FINISHED SIZES OF EMBROIDERIES

Small woven square motif: ⅝in (1.5cm) square

Large woven triangles motif: ¾in (2cm) square

YOU WILL NEED

Note: Quantities are per embroidery.

¼in (5mm) gingham / mini check, one 4in (10cm) square

Stranded cotton floss, one colour to match either the lighter or darker squares in the gingham, working with three strands in the needle

INSTRUCTIONS

Note: Use one colour to embroider each motif, dictated by the colour of the your centre square – if it's the lightest square, use your palest floss; if it's the darkest square, use the darker floss.

SMALL WOVEN SQUARE MOTIF

1 In the corners only, embroider DCSs.

2 Then, around the centre, weave a woven square. Weave two circuits in total.

LARGE WOVEN TRIANGLES MOTIF

1 Stitch a DCS in the centre.

2 Two squares up and below, stitch a DCS; repeat two squares below and on the left- and right-hand sides.

3 Then, around the centre, weave four woven triangles that 'point' inwards, referring to the diagram for positioning. Weave two circuits per triangle.

DIAGRAMS

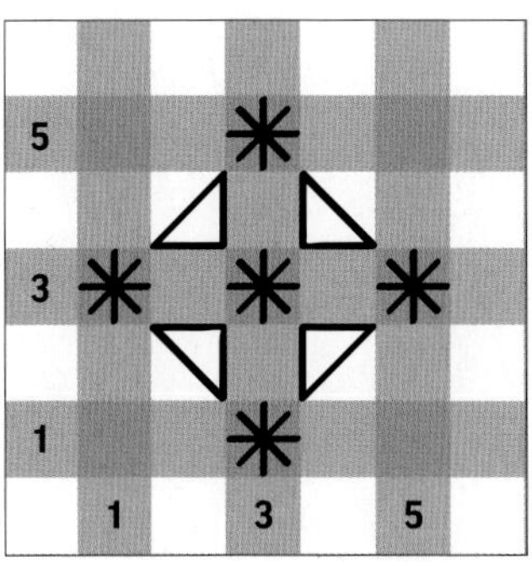

Large woven triangles motif

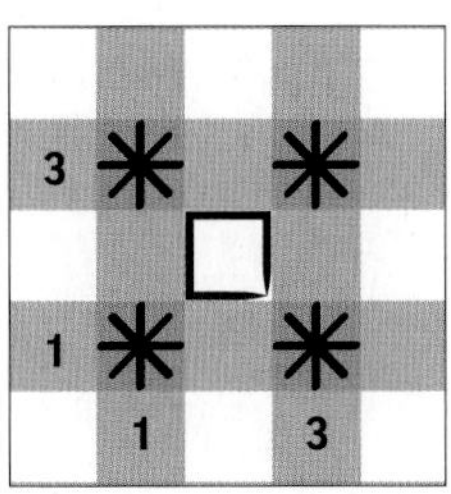

Small woven square motif

SYMBOL KEY

✳ DCS (page 12)

□ Woven squares (page 15)

△ Woven triangles (page 15)

CROSS STITCH CRAZE

Inspirational makes:
I applied this embroidery to a large table mat, using slightly muted yet contrasting floss colours. The mat is simply two rectangles of gingham sewn right sides together, then turned out through a gap left in a side seam before being stitched around the edge. You can work some simple lines of quilting stitches too, if you wish, as I did.

PATTERN NOTES

The complete design is worked over 69 rows of squares, 37 squares across. The centre lines are indicated by red dashed lines, and shows not only the centre lines but also where you will need to mirror the design.

To position your centre lines, fold the gingham fabric into quarters, crease then unfold. Adjust the intersection of the centre lines to ensure it sits centrally over the lightest squares, so all QSs sit on the palest squares. Then, stitch running stitch over your adjusted centre lines to help you position the embroidery. Your lines won't look central at this point, but you can trim the fabric later so they're centred.

FINISHED SIZE OF EMBROIDERY

Approx. 16 x 9in (40.75 x 22.75cm)

YOU WILL NEED

¼in (5mm) gingham / mini check, one 20 x 14in (50.75 x 35.5cm) rectangle

Stranded cotton floss in two colours, working with three strands in the needle – I used red for my first and main shade, then and blue for my secondary QS colour

INSTRUCTIONS

1 Embroider the HCSs in your first colour (I used red). They form a motif (see the red box). Start at the centre then work outwards, repeating the motif. Note the half motifs at the ends of each row.

2 Between the HCS motifs (and the half HCS motifs on the ends of the rows), stitch QSs in your second colour (I used blue).

3 Three squares outside the main design, and working into the lightest squares, stitch a border of SCSs all around in your first colour.

4 Stitch a single SS on the outer edge of each SCS in your first colour. For the corner SCSs, you'll need to add two SS to cover the outer edges.

DIAGRAM: SECTION OF DESIGN

SYMBOL KEY

/	HCS (page 11)
X	SCS (page 11)
⋇	QS (page 12)
|	SS (page 13)

DIAMOND STARBURSTS

Inspirational makes:
This design was worked onto the front of a tote bag. The bag has a simple lined construction, and the handles are faced with waistband interfacing for extra rigidity. I chose to use black floss for a striking, minimalist look, but more shades could be used for a more decorative appearance.

PATTERN NOTES

The complete design is worked over a 45x45 grid of squares. The centre lines are indicated by dashed pink lines, and show where you will need to mirror the design.

To position your centre lines, fold the gingham square into quarters, crease then unfold. Adjust the intersection of the centre lines to ensure it sits centrally over the darkest squares, so that the woven diamonds frame the palest squares. Then, stitch running stitch over your adjusted centre lines to help you position the embroidery. Your lines won't look central at this point, but you can trim the fabric later so they're centred.

FINISHED SIZE OF EMBROIDERY

10½in (26.75cm) square

YOU WILL NEED

¼in (5mm) gingham / mini check, 16in (40.5cm) square

Stranded cotton floss in one colour, working with three strands in the needle – I used black

DIAGRAM: SECTION OF DESIGN

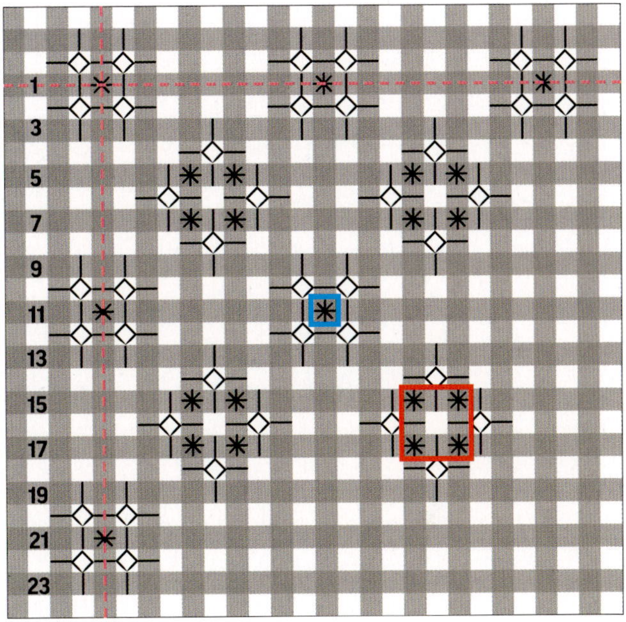

SYMBOL KEY

✳ DCS (page 12)

| SS (page 13)

◇ Woven diamonds (page 14)

INSTRUCTIONS

1 Embroider the DCSs first. They form two motifs – one has a single DCS (see the blue box) and one has four DCSs over a 3x3 grid of squares (see the red box). Start from the centre lines and work outwards, using the diagram as a reference for placement.

2 Next embroider the SSs, working around the two types of motif as shown.

3 Using the SSs, weave four diamonds around each of the motifs as shown. Weave only one circuit for each diamond.

SQUARES IN HEARTS

Inspirational makes:
It goes without saying that this motif sits beautifully on heart-shaped items like decorative hanging hearts. The hearts are 5 x 5½in (12.75 x 14cm). The motif would make a lovely card design too: embroider the heart onto fabric first, cut out the desired shape and hem all around, then adhere to the front of your chosen card.

PATTERN NOTES

The motif is worked over a 15x14 grid of squares and features DCSs and woven squares.

The centre lines are indicated by dashed pink lines. To position your centre lines, fold the gingham square into quarters, crease then unfold. Adjust the intersection of the centre lines to ensure it sits over the darkest squares (if you want woven light squares) or the lightest squares (if you want woven dark squares). Your lines won't look central at this point, but you can trim the fabric later so they're centred.

FINISHED SIZE OF EMBROIDERY

Approx. 3½in (9cm) square

YOU WILL NEED

¼in (5mm) gingham / mini check, one 9in (23cm) square

Stranded cotton floss, in one to two colours that match or coordinate with the gingham, working with three strands in the needle

INSTRUCTIONS

1 Referring to the diagram for positioning, stitch all the DCSs in your first colour.

2 Referring to the diagram once again and using the same or a different colour, add the woven squares between rows 4 and 12. These will frame either the lightest or darkest squares in the gingham, depending on where you placed your centre lines. Weave two circuits per square.

DIAGRAM

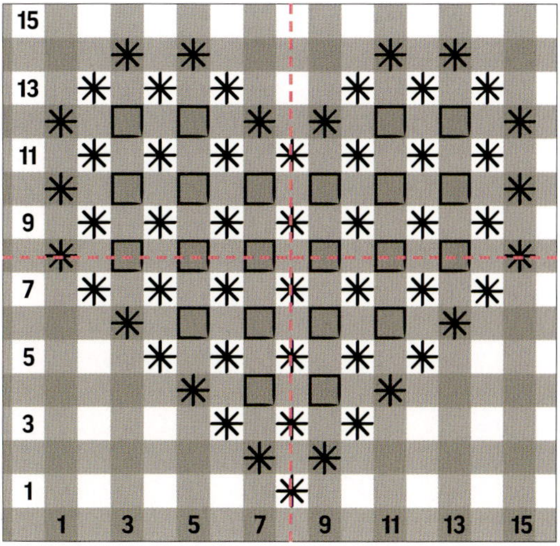

SYMBOL KEY

✳ DCS (page 12)

☐ Woven squares (page 15)

WOVEN CORNERS

Inspirational makes:
I used this embroidery design for the corners of some coasters, constructed by simply sewing the embroidered gingham front to a coordinating backing, with some batting / wadding in between for a little structure. Playing around with the positioning of the embroidery can create a subtle change in the design, leaving you with pale woven squares or darker woven squares.

PATTERN NOTES

The complete design is worked over a 17x17 grid of squares, and features a flower motif (see the purple box) and a square motif (see the red box). The centre lines are indicated by dashed green lines; your centre square, where your running-stitch lines intersect, is 9 squares along and 9 squares up.

To position your centre lines, fold the gingham square into quarters, crease then unfold. Adjust the intersection of the centre lines to ensure it sits centrally over the darkest squares (if you want woven light squares) or the lightest squares (if you want woven dark squares). Then, stitch running stitch over your adjusted centre lines to help you position the embroidery. Your lines won't look central at this point, but you can trim the fabric later so they're centred.

FINISHED SIZE OF EMBROIDERY

Approx. 4in (10cm) wide and 4in (10cm) tall, with the diagonal edge measuring approx. 5¼in (13.25cm)

YOU WILL NEED

¼in (5mm) gingham / mini check, one 7½in (19cm) square

Stranded cotton floss, in two colours, working with three strands in the needle – I used either blue or white for my first colour to match the gingham, and red or green for my second colour as a contrast shade

DIAGRAM

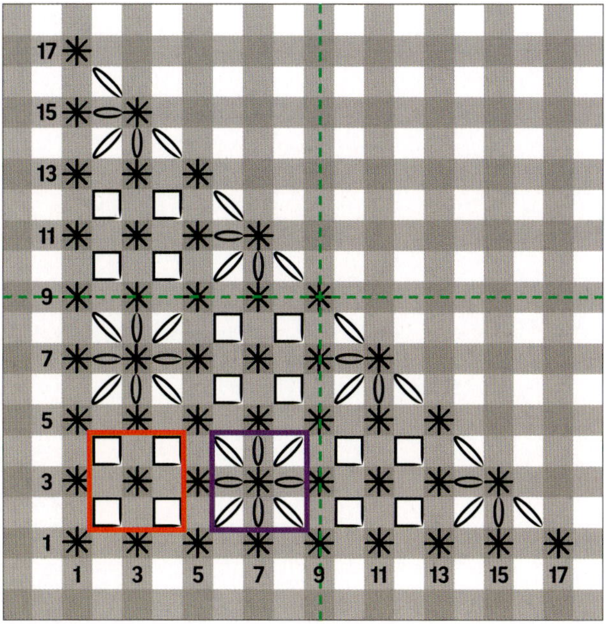

SYMBOL KEY

✳ DCS (page 12)

⬭ Woven ovals (page 16)

☐ Woven squares (page 15)

INSTRUCTIONS

1 Embroider the DCSs in your first colour, starting at the centre where the running-stitch lines intersect and working outwards.

2 Using your second colour, add straight and diagonal woven ovals for the flower motifs (see the purple box). Note these are 'cut in half' along the diagonal right-hand edge. Start with the section in the purple box, and work the two complete motifs first. Weave two circuits per oval.

3 Add the woven squares for the square motif (see the red box), again in your second colour. Weave two circuits per square.

FLOWERBED

Inspirational makes:
I used the embroidery for the central design of a flanged pillow cover, the whole of which measures 19in (48.25cm) square. The embroidery captures the floral theme of the pillow fabric, and is like a tidy little flowerbed in the middle of a meadow filled with lots of pink wildflowers.

PATTERN NOTES

The complete design is worked over a 21x21 grid of squares. The centre lines are indicated by blue dashed lines, and show where you will need to mirror the design.

To position your centre lines, fold the gingham square into quarters, crease then unfold. Adjust the intersection of the centre lines to ensure it sits centrally over the lightest squares (so all your DCSs are placed on the palest squares). Your lines won't look central at this point, but you can trim the fabric later so they're centred. Then, stitch running stitch over your adjusted centre lines to help you position the embroidery.

FINISHED SIZE OF EMBROIDERY

5in (12.75cm) square

YOU WILL NEED

¼in (5mm) gingham / mini check, one 9in (22.75cm) square

Stranded cotton floss, in five colours, working with three strands in the needle – I used for green for my DCS 'leaves', and lilac, yellow, blue and red for my woven-cross 'flowers'

INSTRUCTIONS

1 Working from the centre (where your running-stitch lines intersect) outwards, stitch all the DCSs on the palest squares using your first colour (mine was green). These are your flowerbed 'leaves'.

2 Using your second colour, now work woven crosses in between the DCSs, for your 'flowers' – space them so that you can create a repeating pattern of colour as shown. Repeat with the remaining three colours.

DIAGRAM: SECTION OF DESIGN

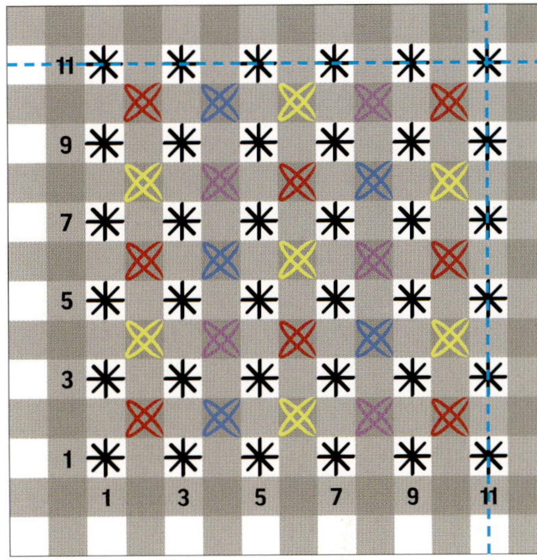

SYMBOL KEY

✳ DCS (page 12)

⊠ Woven cross (page 17)

WOVEN TOWER

Inspirational makes:

This design adds some fun to this tote bag, which has a simple lined construction and rigid, faced handles. As there are lots of stitches, I decided to use just the one colour – cream – for the whole design, to create harmony; however, more colours could be used. For example, depending on the gingham, all the DCSs could be stitched with a colour, and then cream used only for the woven stitches.

PATTERN NOTES

The complete design is worked over a 29x27 grid of squares.

To position your centre lines, fold the gingham square into quarters, crease then unfold. Adjust the intersection of the centre lines to ensure it sits centrally over the darkest squares (so all your DCSs are placed on the darkest squares). Then, stitch running stitch over your adjusted centre lines to help you position the embroidery. Your lines won't look central at this point, but you can trim the fabric later so they're centred.

As the design lines up along the left-hand edge, if you wish you can add an extra line of running stitches 2in (5cm) from this edge to use as another guide line.

FINISHED SIZE OF EMBROIDERY

Approx. 7¼ x 7in (18.5 x 17.75cm)

YOU WILL NEED

¼in (5mm) gingham / mini check, one 10½in (26.75cm) square

Two skeins of stranded cotton floss in one colour, working with three stands in the needle - I used cream

DIAGRAM

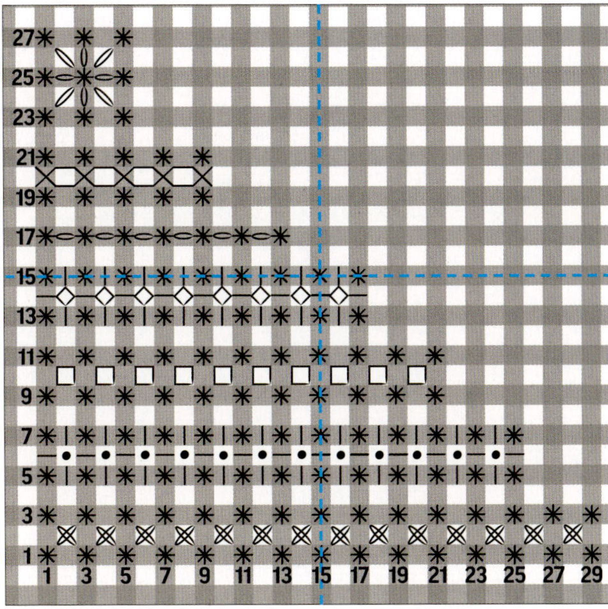

SYMBOL KEY

- DCS (page 12)
- Woven cross (page 17)
- SS (page 13)
- FK (page 13)
- Woven squares (page 15)
- Woven diamonds (page 14)
- Woven ovals (page 16)
- Continuous line (pages 18–19)

INSTRUCTIONS

1 Referring to the diagram for placement, stitch in all the DCSs.

2 Working from bottom to top, and again referring to the diagram throughout, add in the remaining stitches – woven crosses, SSs, FKs, woven squares, woven diamonds, woven ovals and continuous lines. For the woven stitches, work two circuits in total.

LATTICE

Inspirational makes:
With just two stitches, but lots of colours, a simple table cloth can be transformed into an intricate homeware you'll be proud to have on show. The lattice design could also look great on table mats, and a single woven cross motif could be stitched onto a coaster for a colourful table set.

PATTERN NOTES

The complete design is worked over a 135x135 grid of squares. The diagrams on page 34 show only a section of the DCS border and the woven cross motif, and these are repeated to create the overall design.

The woven cross motifs, when 'tiled' together, create a lattice-like effect.

To position your centre lines, fold the gingham square into quarters, crease then unfold. Adjust the intersection of the centre lines to ensure it sits centrally over the darkest squares (so all your QSs are placed on the darkest squares). Then, stitch running stitch over your adjusted centre lines to help you position the embroidery.

Your lines won't look central at this point, but you can trim the fabric later so they're centred.

YOU WILL NEED

¼in (5mm) gingham / mini check, 40in (101.5cm) square

Stranded cotton floss in as many colours as you like, working with three strands in the needle – I used around 20 different colours, and used them several times throughout the embroidery in the border and woven cross motifs to create cohesion

FINISHED SIZE OF EMBROIDERY

34in (86.5cm) square

Turn over for instructions >>>

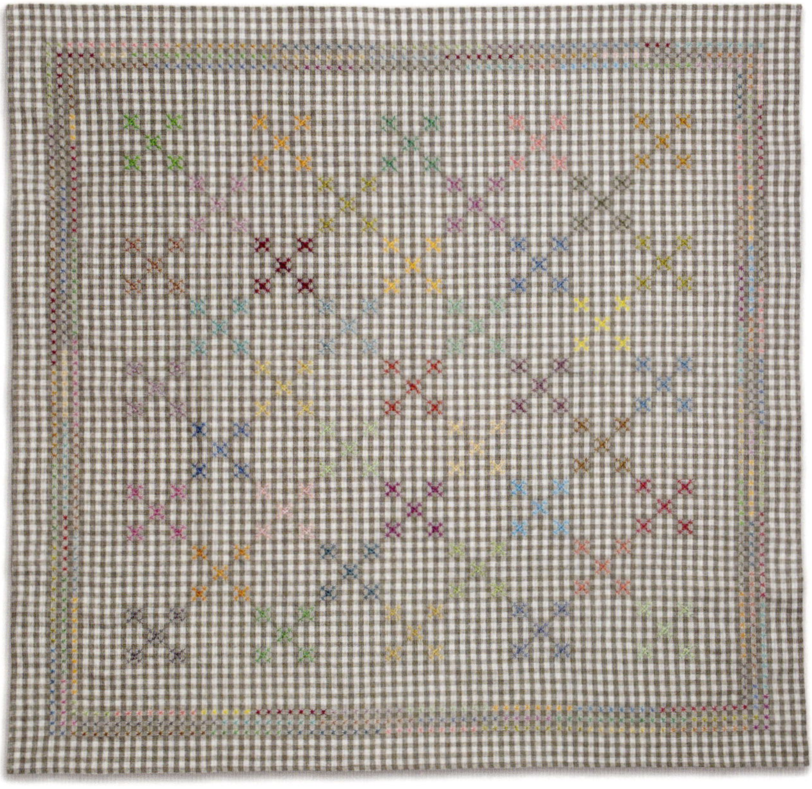

INSTRUCTIONS

Note: I recommend using a hoop while you embroider, as this is a large design to stitch and it could easily distort.

1 The first of the woven cross motifs is stitched over the intersecting central lines, and it's from here you work outwards and add the rest of the motifs. To stitch the first motif, select your first colour then start by stitching its centre (see the pink box in the woven-cross diagram): there are four DCSs in the corners of a 3x3 grid of squares, with a woven cross in the middle of them.

2 Stitch the rest of elements in the woven cross motif, as shown. The complete motif should cover an 11x11 grid of squares.

3 Working from the centre of the gingham outwards, either in columns or rows, add the rest of the motifs in the same way. There are 41 woven cross motifs across the whole design, with 23 squares between the central woven crosses of two adjacent motifs (counting horizontally and vertically). Change colours for each motif, and try to make sure you don't place the same colours next to each other. You will end up with a lattice-like spread of woven-cross motifs, upon completion.

4 Now for the border. Count 15 squares out from the central woven cross of one outer woven cross motif; square 15 is where your inner line of DCSs will sit. Changing colours every 4 to 13 squares (this can be completely up to you), stitch the inner border line with DCSs all the way around the woven cross lattice.

5 Count two squares out from the inner border, and repeat the process of adding a line of DCSs all around the inner border.

6 Repeat step 5 to add a final border around the design.

DIAGRAMS: REPEATS

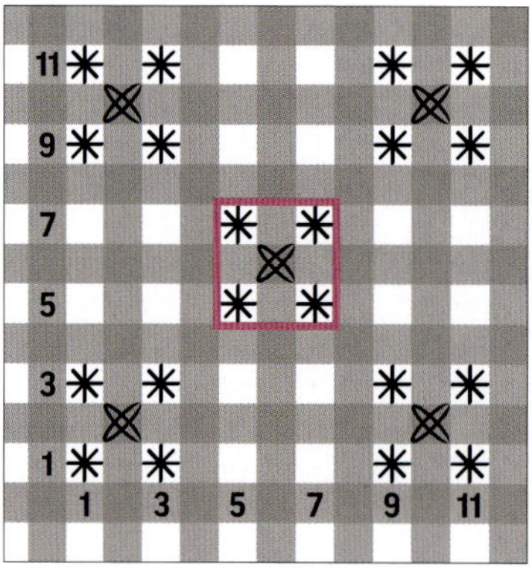

Woven cross motif

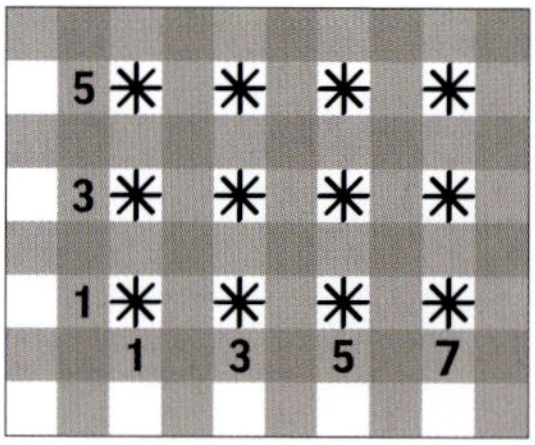

DCS border

SYMBOL KEY

✳ DCS (page 12)

⊗ Woven cross (page 17)

HEARTS & FLOWERS

Inspirational makes:
The flowers and hearts in this design have been stitched on alternating flags of a length of an eight-pennant bunting. However, you could embroider them in a row in an alternating order around the hem of a skirt or the edge of a table cloth.

FLOWER MOTIF

PATTERN NOTES

The diagram, right, shows a single repeat of the flower motif, which is made using just two stitches – DCSs and woven ovals. The motif is worked over a 5x9 grid of squares, and the centre square of the motif where your running-stitch lines will intersect is 3 squares across and 5 squares up (see the blue box in the diagram, right).

To position your centre lines, fold the gingham square into quarters, crease then unfold. Adjust the intersection of the centre lines to ensure it sits centrally over the lightest squares (so all your DCSs are placed on the palest squares). Then, stitch running stitch over your adjusted centre lines to help you position the embroidery. Your lines won't look central at this point, but you can trim the fabric later so they're centred.

FINISHED SIZE OF EMBROIDERY

1½ x 2¾in (3.75 x 7cm)

YOU WILL NEED

¼in (5mm) gingham / mini check, one 5in (12.75cm) square

Stranded cotton floss in black, working with three strands in the needle

DIAGRAM

SYMBOL KEY

✳ DCS (page 12)

⬭ Woven ovals (page 16)

INSTRUCTIONS

1 Referring to the diagram for placement, embroider a grid of 3x5 DCSs over a 5x9 grid of the fabric, working on the lightest squares.

2 Now weave ovals between the relevant DCSs to create the leaves, stem and petals. Weave two circuits per oval.

HEART MOTIF

PATTERN NOTES

The diagram, right, shows a single repeat of the heart motif, which is made using just one stitch – DCSs.

The motif is worked over a 7x6 grid of squares, and its centre is 4 squares across and 3 squares up (see the pink box in the diagram, right).

To position your centre lines, fold the gingham square into quarters, crease then unfold. Adjust the intersection of the centre lines to ensure it sits centrally over the lightest squares. Then, stitch running stitch over your adjusted centre lines to help you position the embroidery. Your lines won't look central at this point, but you can trim the fabric later so they're centred.

FINISHED SIZE OF EMBROIDERY

Approx. 2¼ x 2in (5.75 x 5cm)

YOU WILL NEED

¼in (5mm) gingham / mini check, one 4in (10cm) square

Stranded cotton floss in black, working with three strands in the needle

INSTRUCTIONS

1 Referring to the diagram for placement, start by stitching the DCSs on the lightest squares – the three on the vertical centre line and the two on each side.

3 Add the remaining DCSs on the dark squares, finishing with DCSs on the mid-tone squares.

DIAGRAM

SYMBOL KEY

✳ DCS (page 12)

FLORAL HEDGEROW

Inspirational makes:
I used this embroidery for a drawstring bag measuring 9½ x 8½in (24.25 x 21.5cm). It's a simple lined construction with a square-bottomed base and a drawstring channel at the top. The fabric for the drawstring casing was chosen to coordinate with the floss colours in the embroidery. The design could easily be repeated across multiple items – for example the hem of a garment, or as a border around the edge of a cloth or mat.

PATTERN NOTES

The motif is worked over a 5x5 grid of squares and features DCSs and woven ovals.

To position your centre lines, fold the gingham square into quarters, crease then unfold. Adjust the intersection of the central lines to ensure it sits centrally over the darkest squares. Then, stitch running stitch over your adjusted centre lines to help you position the embroidery. Your lines won't look central at this point, but you can trim the fabric later so they're centred.

FINISHED SIZE OF EMBROIDERY

Approx. 1⅛in (3cm) square

YOU WILL NEED

¼in (5mm) gingham / mini check, one 3in (7.5cm) square

Stranded cotton floss, in two to three colours, working with three strands in the needle – I used green, pink and purple

INSTRUCTIONS

1 Referring to the diagram for positioning, stitch all the DCSs in your first colour (I used green). For the drawstring bag opposite, I worked three rows of DCSs on the darkest squares. If you wish to create a border like this, note that the number of DCSs in each row or column must be divisible by five.

2 Referring to the diagram once again and using your remaining colour(s), add the woven ovals around the central DCS of each 3x3 grouping of DCSs to create a flower motif. Weave two circuits per oval.

DIAGRAM: REPEAT

SYMBOL KEY

✳ DCS (page 12)

⬭ Woven ovals (page 16)

WOVEN EXPLOSION

Inspirational makes:
I used my motifs for hoop art, using 3in (7.5cm) hoops that were bound with a coordinating 1½in (3.75cm) wide strip of fabric. Make several to hang together on a wall, or use festive colours so that you can to hang them on a Christmas tree. The size of the motif means it would look great worked on the pocket of an apron or another garment.

PATTERN NOTES

The motif is embroidered over a 7x7 grid of squares featuring DCSs, woven ovals and a woven cross at the centre. The centre square of the design, where your running-stitch lines will intersect, is 4 squares across and 4 squares up (see the red box in the diagram, right).

To position your centre lines, fold the gingham square into quarters, crease then unfold. Adjust the intersection of the centre lines to ensure it sits over the darkest squares (so all your DCSs are placed on the lightest squares). Then, stitch running stitch over your adjusted centre lines to help you position the embroidery. Your lines won't look central at this point, but you can trim the fabric later so they're centred.

FINISHED SIZE

3in (7.5cm) in diameter per hoop

YOU WILL NEED

¼in (5mm) gingham / mini check, one 6in (15.25cm) square

Stranded cotton floss, in one to three colours that match or coordinate with the gingham, working with three strands in the needle

INSTRUCTIONS

1 Using your first colour, stitch a 7x7 grid of DCSs on the lightest squares.

2 In the centre, and using the central four DCSs to weave around, make a woven cross with either the first or second colour.

3 In each outermost 'corner' of the four DCSs, weave three ovals that 'point' towards the centre with the first, second or third colour. Weave two circuits per oval.

DIAGRAM

SYMBOL KEY

✳ DCS (page 12)

⊗ Woven cross (page 17)

⬭ Woven ovals (page 16)

TESSELLATING QUINTETS

Inspirational makes:

There's something about the contrast of the magenta thread on the teal gingham that adds a modern twist to this pincushion. The square I embroidered on was cut on the bias, then stabilized for structure while I stitched; so, although I stitched as I would for other designs, the fabric creates the diagonal effect. The pincushion is approx. 7in (17.75cm) square. If you don't want a diagonal effect, the middle section of the motif could easily be repeated and used for a decorative border on lots of items, such as the hem of a skirt or dress.

PATTERN NOTES

The complete design is worked over 25 rows of squares, 35 squares across, using QSs, SSs and HCSs. The centre lines are indicated by the blue dashed lines; the vertical centre line is where you will need to mirror the design.

To position your centre lines, fold the gingham square into quarters, crease then unfold. Adjust the intersection of the central lines to ensure it sits centrally over the darkest or lightest squares – the diagram shows the latter. Then, stitch running stitch over your adjusted centre lines to help you position the embroidery. Your lines won't look central at this point, but you can trim the fabric later so they're centred.

FINISHED SIZE OF EMBROIDERY

Approx. 8 x 6½in (20.25 x 16.5cm)

YOU WILL NEED

¼in (5mm) gingham / mini check, one 12in (30.5cm) square

Stranded cotton floss, in a contrasting colour, working with three strands in the needle

INSTRUCTIONS

1 Referring to the diagram for positioning, stitch all the QSs.

2 Referring to the diagram again for placement, embroider all the horizontal lines with SS. It's possible to stitch these with a running-stitch motion.

3 Finish by embroidering all the HSCs, paying close attention to the diagram to ensure the stitches are all at the correct angle.

DIAGRAM: SECTION OF DESIGN

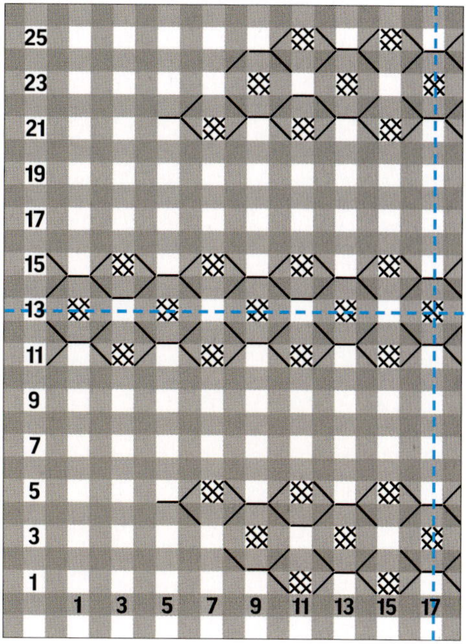

SYMBOL KEY

QS (page 12)

| SS (page 13)

/ HCS (page 11)

FLOWERS IN HEARTS

Inspirational makes:
It's only fitting to have this design on a heart-shaped item! I used mine on decorative hanging hearts. The largest heart, left, is 6 x 5¾in (15.25 x 14.5cm); the other, smaller hearts are 5 x 5½in (12.75 x 14cm). The motif would equally work well on the front of a card (stitch onto fabric first, cut out, hem then adhere to the card's front) or even the pocket on a pair of trousers.

PATTERN NOTES

The motif is worked over a 15x14 grid of squares and features DCSs and woven ovals. The centre is indicated by the red box in the diagram, right.

To position your centre lines, fold the gingham square into quarters, crease then unfold. Adjust the intersection of the centre lines to ensure it sits centrally over the darkest squares. Then, stitch running stitch over your adjusted centre lines to help you position the embroidery. Your lines won't look central at this point, but you can trim the fabric later so they're centred.

FINISHED SIZE OF EMBROIDERY

Approx. 3½in (9cm) square

YOU WILL NEED

¼in (5mm) gingham / mini check, one 9in (23cm) square

Stranded cotton floss, in one to three colours, working with three strands in the needle

INSTRUCTIONS

1 Referring to the diagram for positioning, stitch all the DCSs in your first colour.

2 Referring to the diagram once again and using your remaining colour(s), add the woven ovals between rows 5 and 13 to create flower shapes. Weave two circuits per oval.

DIAGRAM

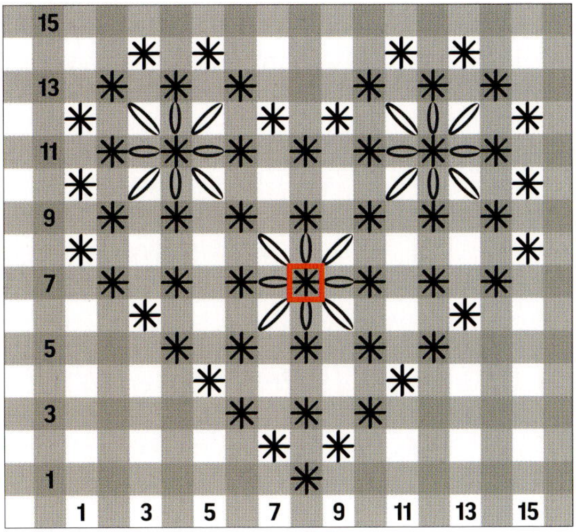

SYMBOL KEY

✳ DCS (page 12)

⬭ Woven ovals (page 16)

QUINTET STITCH DIAMOND

Inspirational makes:
I used this embroidery for a drawstring bag measuring 9½ x 8½in (24.25 x 21.5cm). It's a simple lined construction with a square-bottomed base and a drawstring channel at the top. The fabric for the drawstring casing was chosen to coordinate with the floss colours in the embroidery. The design would equally work on a pillow front, and could be easily extended on all sides for a larger motif.

PATTERN NOTES

The diagram, right, features the whole motif. It's stitched with a mix of QSs and woven diamonds over a 21x21 grid of squares, positioned cleverly to create a diamond shape. The centre is 11 squares across and 11 squares up; see the intersection of the yellow dashed lines.

To position your centre lines, fold the gingham square into quarters, crease then unfold. Adjust the intersection of the central lines to ensure it sits centrally over the lightest squares. Then, stitch running stitch over your adjusted centre lines to help you position the embroidery design. Your lines won't look central at this point, but you can trim the fabric later so they're centred.

FINISHED SIZE OF EMBROIDERY

Approx. 5in (12.75cm) square

YOU WILL NEED

¼in (5mm) gingham / mini check, at least 8in (20cm) square

Stranded cotton floss, in four colours, working with three strands in the needle – I used yellow, red, blue and green

DIAGRAM

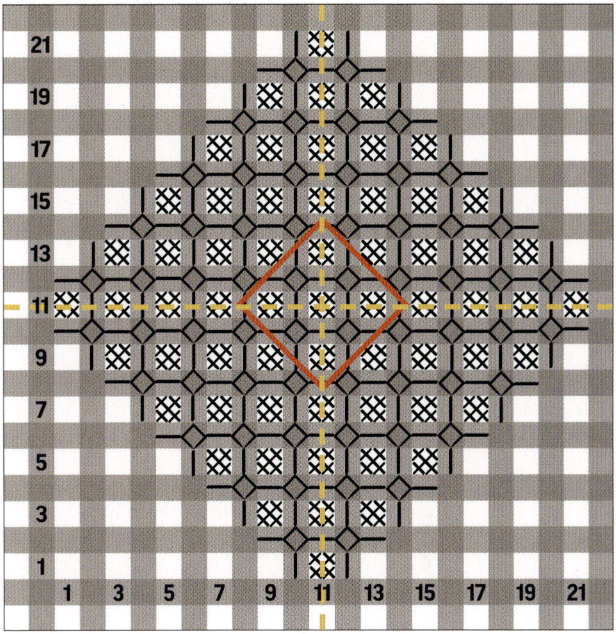

SYMBOL KEY

※ QS (page 12)

| SS (page 13)

◇ Woven diamonds (page 14)

INSTRUCTIONS

1 Start by stitching a 'diamond' of five QSs at the centre of the gingham using your first colour (see the orange box in the diagram above) – I used yellow floss.

2 Working from the centre outwards, complete the remaining diamond-shaped rounds of QSs in the following colour order: second, third, first, second.

3 Stitch the horizontal and vertical SSs between the QSs with your fourth floss colour.

4 Using the SSs and with the fourth colour, weave the woven diamonds to finish the embroidery design. Weave one circuit per diamond.

STARBURST HEARTS

Inspirational makes:
This motif works beautifully on bunting, made from scratch here using a simple construction of two pieces of fabric stitched right sides together, around the bottom and sides only, then turned out; the fabric tape is then wrapped and stitched around the top raw edges. The motif could easily be repeated in a row if desired, for example around the hem of a table cloth or apron, or used singly for a coaster or purse.

PATTERN NOTES

The diagram, right, shows the motif – a starburst-like design, with little heart shapes in the corners, made entirely in QSs. The motif is worked over a 7x7 square grid, and the centre square of the design, where your two running-stitch lines will intersect, is 4 squares across and 4 squares up (see the orange box in the diagram).

To position your centre lines, fold the gingham square into quarters, crease then unfold. Adjust the intersection of the centre lines to ensure it sits centrally over the lightest squares. Then, stitch running stitch over your adjusted centre lines to help you position the embroidery. Your lines won't look central at this point, but you can trim the fabric later so they're centred.

FINISHED SIZE OF EMBROIDERY

2in (5cm) square

YOU WILL NEED

¼in (5mm) gingham / mini check, one 5in (12.75cm) square

Stranded cotton floss, in two to three colours, working with three strands in the needle - I used two colours, as one is variegated and creates an extra tone

INSTRUCTIONS

1 Stitch the central QS in your first colour.

2 Around the centre square, stitch four QSs, one touching each corner of the central stitch, using your second colour.

3 Referring to the diagram, stitch four more QSs around the centre stitches in a diagonal shape – at the top and bottom and on the left- and right-hand sides – using either your second colour or a third one. Note that if you're using a variegated floss like I am for the second colour, you may not need a third colour – see the photograph, right.

4 Return to your first colour to work three QSs in each corner, forming little V-shapes that 'point' towards the centre as shown.

DIAGRAM

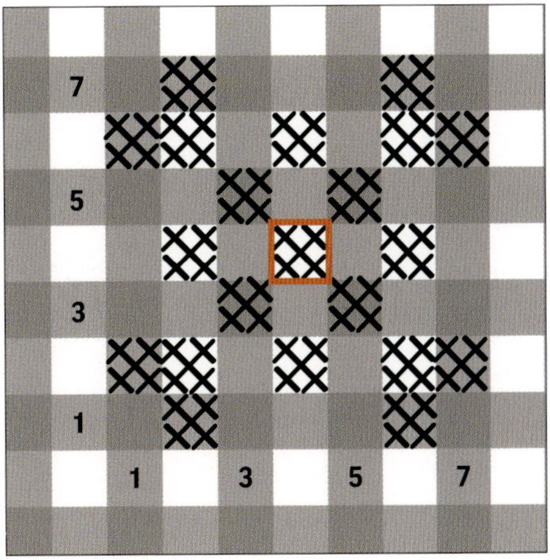

SYMBOL KEY

※ QS (page 12)

OUTLINED SQUARES

Inspirational makes:
This design lends itself to so many different things – as a stand-alone motif on a bookmark, like the example here, to repeating rows on the hems of garments. You could even adapt the design to use as a border around a table cloth or table set.

PATTERN NOTES

The motif is 3 squares wide, and is repeated over 4 rows (see the pink box in the diagram, right). It ends with the continuous lines crossing between two DCSs.

To position your centre lines, fold the gingham fabric into quarters, crease then unfold. Adjust your the intersection of the central lines to ensure it sits over either the lightest or darkest squares. Then, stitch running stitch over your adjusted centre lines to help you position the embroidery. Your lines won't look central at this point, but you can trim the fabric later so they're centred.

FINISHED SIZE OF EMBROIDERY

Approx. 1½ x 11½ (3.75 x 29.25cm), based on a row of eight repeats worked across 33 squares of ¼in (5mm) gingham / mini check

YOU WILL NEED

¼in (5mm) gingham / mini check, minimum one 2 x 3in (5 x 7.5cm) piece - this is for one repeat

Stranded cotton floss, in one to two colours, working with three strands in the needle

INSTRUCTIONS

1 Referring to the diagram for positioning, stitch all the DCSs in your first colour – they should sit on the lightest or darkest squares. I start at the centre and work outwards in either direction with my stitching; this way I can always end up with the same number of stitches either side of the centre stitch.

2 Referring to the diagram once again and using your first or second colour, work the continuous line from bottom to top, as explained on page 18. Weave just one circuit in total.

DIAGRAM: REPEAT

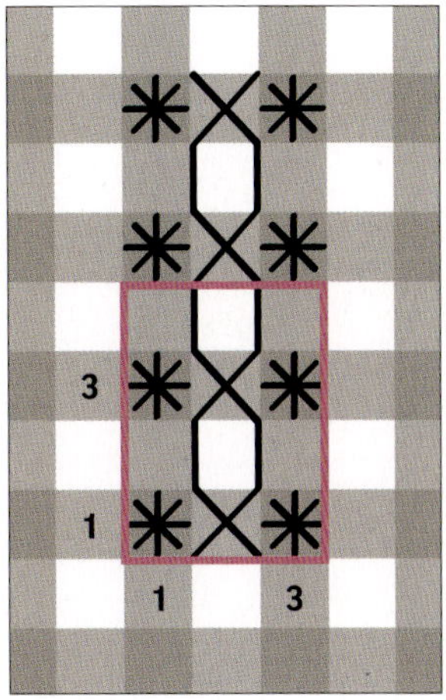

SYMBOL KEY

✳ DCS (page 12)

⌐_ Continuous line (pages 18–19)

WOVEN ZIGZAGS

Inspirational makes:

I chose to embellish an old blouse with this design. I embroidered from the bottom of the motif upwards; I worked this way as I wanted to ensure the 'point' of the motif of the design sat in my desired position, then I could work as many of the repeats above this as required. When I reached the neckline I had the option to stop the design in a straight line or to work it to fit the slight curve.

This motif could also work well on the front of a tote bag.

PATTERN NOTES

The complete design is worked over 39 rows of squares, 21 squares across, using DCSs, SSs and woven diamonds. The centre line is indicated by the dashed line, and shows where you will need to mirror the design.

The design can be extended or shortened, by adding or removing the repeat between rows 8 to 15 (see the pink box). Ensuring you are working from the centre line too, I advise that you work from the bottom upwards, as the number of embroidered squares starts with 1, then increases symmetrically.

To position your centre lines, fold the fabric in half lengthways, centring one of the stripes which contains the darkest or lightest squares – the diagram shows the latter. Then, stitch running stitch over your centre lines to help you position the embroidery. Your lines won't look central at this point, but you can trim the fabric later so they're centred.

FINISHED SIZE OF EMBROIDERY

Approx. 5 x 8½in (12.75 x 21.5cm)

YOU WILL NEED

¼in (5mm) gingham / mini check, one 8 x 11in (20.5 x 28cm) piece

Two skeins of stranded cotton floss in one colour, working with three strands in the needle – I used brown

INSTRUCTIONS

1 Referring to the diagram for positioning, stitch all the DCSs.

2 Referring to the diagram for direction, embroider all the SSs – note all the odd numbered rows (apart from row 1) have vertical SSs, and all the even rows have horizontal SSs.

3 Using the SSs as their base, and on every even row, weave the woven diamonds. Weave one circuit per diamond.

DIAGRAM: SECTION OF DESIGN

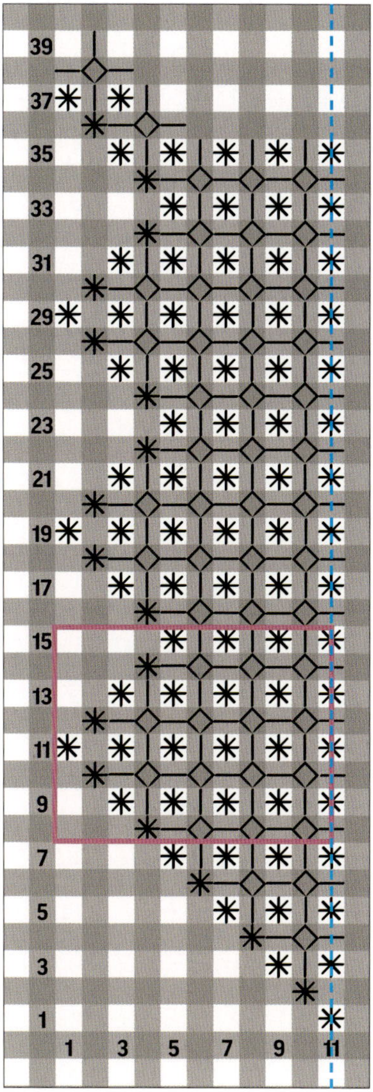

SYMBOL KEY

✳ DCS (page 12)

| SS (page 13)

◇ Woven diamonds (page 14)

BRODERIE SUISSE TRIBUTE

Inspirational makes:
Although 'broderie suisse' is essentially another name for gingham embroidery, it's marked by its particular use of red gingham, and white and red threads. I used the design on a 9in (23cm) square pincushion, which has a simple bagged-out construction with stuffing inside. The design could easily be enlarged for a sofa pillow or bag front, or reduced in scale for a pocket motif.

PATTERN NOTES

The complete design is worked over a 21x21 grid of squares, using DCSs, SSs, woven diamonds and woven squares. It's essentially a square within a square, with a smaller square motif of DCSs, SSs and woven diamonds in the centre, then a border of DCSs and woven squares around it. The centre square is indicated by the intersection of the yellow dashed lines.

To position your centre lines, fold the gingham square into quarters, crease then unfold. Adjust the intersection of the central lines to ensure it sits over the darkest or lightest squares – the diagram shows the former, to ensure the woven diamonds and squares frame the palest squares. Then, stitch running stitch over your adjusted centre lines to help you position the embroidery. Your lines won't look central at this point, but you can trim the fabric later so they're centred.

FINISHED SIZE OF EMBROIDERY

Approx. 6¾in (17cm) square

YOU WILL NEED

¼in (5mm) gingham / mini check, one 11in (28cm) square

Stranded cotton floss, in red and white, working with three strands in the needle

DIAGRAM

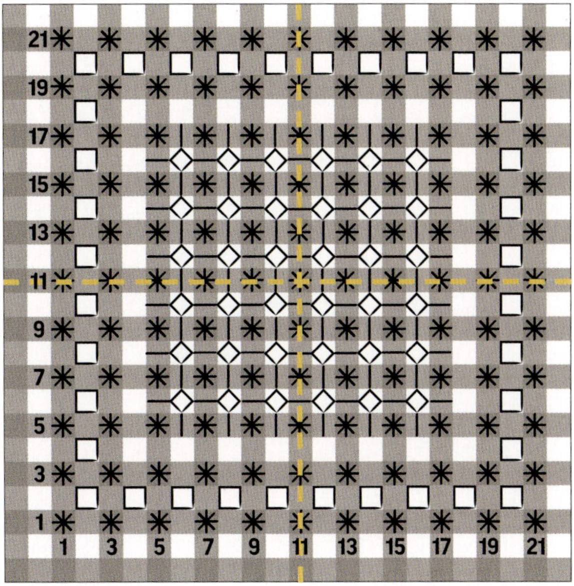

SYMBOL KEY

✳ DCS (page 12)

| SS (page 13)

◇ Woven diamonds (page 14)

□ Woven squares (page 15)

INSTRUCTIONS

1 Referring to the diagram for positioning, stitch all the DCSs.

2 From 5 squares across to 17 squares across, and from rows 5 to 17, embroider the SSs between the DCSs – I used white for these. Note all the even rows have horizontal SSs, and all the odd rows have vertical SSs. Leave an empty square between the SSs to allow space for the woven diamonds.

3 In the empty squares, add the woven diamonds, weaving into the SSs. I used red for all the weaving stitches. Work one circuit only.

4 Leaving an empty 'border' around the central square design, finish by stitching the woven square border all around, inside the outer ring of DCSs. Work two circuits for emphasis.

QUINTET TULIPS

Inspirational makes:
I used this embroidery for a drawstring bag measuring 9½ x 8½in (24.25 x 21.5cm). It's a simple lined construction with a square-bottomed base and a drawstring channel at the top. The fabric for the drawstring casing was chosen to coordinate with the floss colours in the embroidery. The design would look wonderful on a large pocket, or make a lovely decorative centre of a table mat.

PATTERN NOTES

The diagram, right, features the whole motif. It's stitched using a combination of DCSs, SSs, QSs and woven diamonds, and is designed to create the illusion of tulips 'growing' from a decorative square centre. The motif is worked over a 17x17 grid of squares, and the centre is indicated by the intersection of the red dashed lines.

To position your centre lines, fold the gingham square into quarters, crease then unfold. Adjust the intersection of the centre lines to ensure it sits over the lightest squares (so all your DCSs are placed on the palest squares). Your lines won't look central at this point, but you can trim the fabric later so they're centred. Then, stitch running stitch over your adjusted centre lines to help you position the embroidery.

FINISHED SIZE OF EMBROIDERY

Approx. 4in (10cm) square

YOU WILL NEED

¼in (5mm) gingham / mini check, at least 8in (20cm) square

Stranded cotton floss in three colours, working with three strands in the needle - I used green, variegated red and gold

DIAGRAM

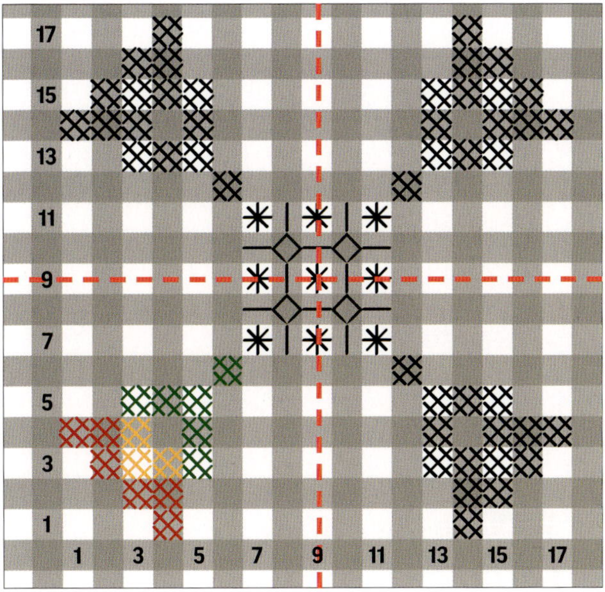

SYMBOL KEY

✳ DCS (page 12)

| SS (page 13)

QS (page 12)

◇ Woven diamonds (page 14)

INSTRUCTIONS

1 Start by stitching a group of nine DCSs in your first colour (I used green) at the centre of the gingham, working over a 5x5 grid of squares.

2 Referring to the diagram for placement and direction, and using your second colour (I used variegated red), embroider the vertical and horizontal SS lines between the DCSs.

3 Using the SSs and continuing with your second colour, weave the woven diamonds around the centre of the design. Weave two circuits per diamond.

4 Referring to the diagram and with your first colour, embroider a QS above each corner of the DCS 5x5 grid of squares (four QSs in total).

5 Still using the first colour, and starting one diagonal square from the QSs made in the previous step, embroider five more QSs at each corner, forming chevron shapes.

6 Referring to the diagram above, change to your third colour (I used gold), then embroider three QSs in a chevron shape.

7 Complete the design by embroidering two little chevron shapes – made up of three QSs – at the corners in your second colour, referring to the diagram for positioning.

PRIMROSE ROWS

Inspirational makes:
This design would work wonderfully as a decorative trim on the bottom hem of a garment or the top edge of a pocket; it could also be repeated around the perimeter of a table set or table cloth, for a delicate floral edging. I used the design for the stand-alone, central motif of a decorative bird: I embroidered across 25 squares of my chosen gingham, cut out a bird shape from it and another piece of the same gingham with a hand-made template, sewed the two bird shapes RS together, then turned out the bird before stuffing then closing up the gap by hand.

PATTERN NOTES

The repeat for the motif is worked over a 5x5 grid (see the pink box), using DCSs and woven squares. Each repeat is essentially a flower shape with DCSs around it.

To position your centre lines, fold the gingham fabric into quarters, crease then unfold. Adjust the intersection of the central lines to ensure it sits over the darkest or lightest of squares – the diagram shows the latter. Then, stitch running stitch over your adjusted centre lines to help you position the embroidery design. Your lines won't look central at this point, but you can trim the fabric later so they're centred.

FINISHED SIZE OF EMBROIDERY

Approx. 1½ x 5in (3.75 x 12.75cm), based on a row of flowers worked across 25 squares of ¼in (5mm) gingham / mini check

YOU WILL NEED

¼in (5mm) gingham / mini check, one 8 x 4in (20 x 10cm) piece

Stranded cotton floss, in two to three colours, working with three strands in the needle

INSTRUCTIONS

1 Referring to the diagram for positioning, stitch all the DCSs – use your first colour for all the DCSs in rows 1 and 5, but alternate between your first and second colours for row 3.

2 Starting directly under the central DCS of each motif (rather than from a corner stitch of a DCS), work four woven squares around the central DCS, adapting the stitching slightly as shown. Weave one circuit per 'square'. Anchoring the thread directly underneath the DCS at the centre of the grid should pull the thread slightly and make it taper, creating more of petal-like effect and forming a neat flower.

DIAGRAM

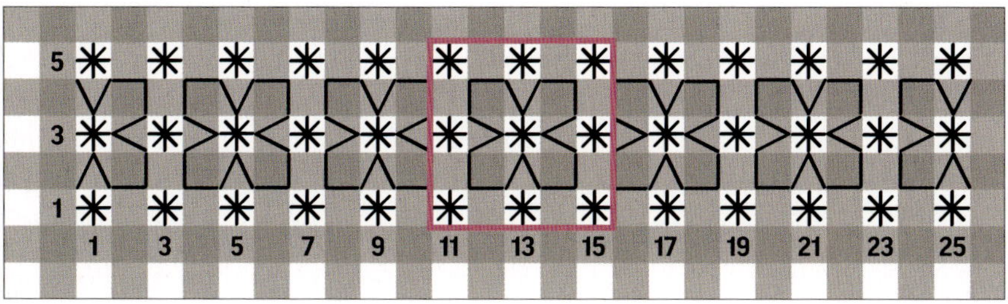

SYMBOL KEY

✳ DCS (page 12)

☐ Woven squares (page 15)

GINGHAM TEMPLATE

Fun as it is to create as we embroider, sometimes the ideas are just so many and come too fast to stitch them all. When this happens, I like to plan my designs on squared paper. Drawing your design before stitching is also ideal if you want to decide how big a motif you'd like to stitch, and how it will look on the darker or lighter squares of your fabric.

Use this ¼in (5mm) square gingham template to start creating your own embroidery designs, using the symbols for the various stitches on page 20.

You can use coloured pens and pencils (or just black) for drawing your designs, and you can draw with pens that have thicker or finer nibs to represent the number of embroidery strands to use or how many 'circuits' to work for woven designs – whatever works for you.

If you need more space, you can copy and tile this template onto a larger sheet of paper; you could also use a gridded notebook or dotted paper too.